The Kagai in Kyoto
– Legendary Beauty of Geiko and Maiko
Photo: MIZOBUCHI Hiroshi

京都の花街

―芸妓・舞妓の伝統美―

写真 溝縁ひろし

光村推古書院

祇園甲部 | Gion Kobu

祇園
新地
歌舞練

宮川町 | Miyagawacho

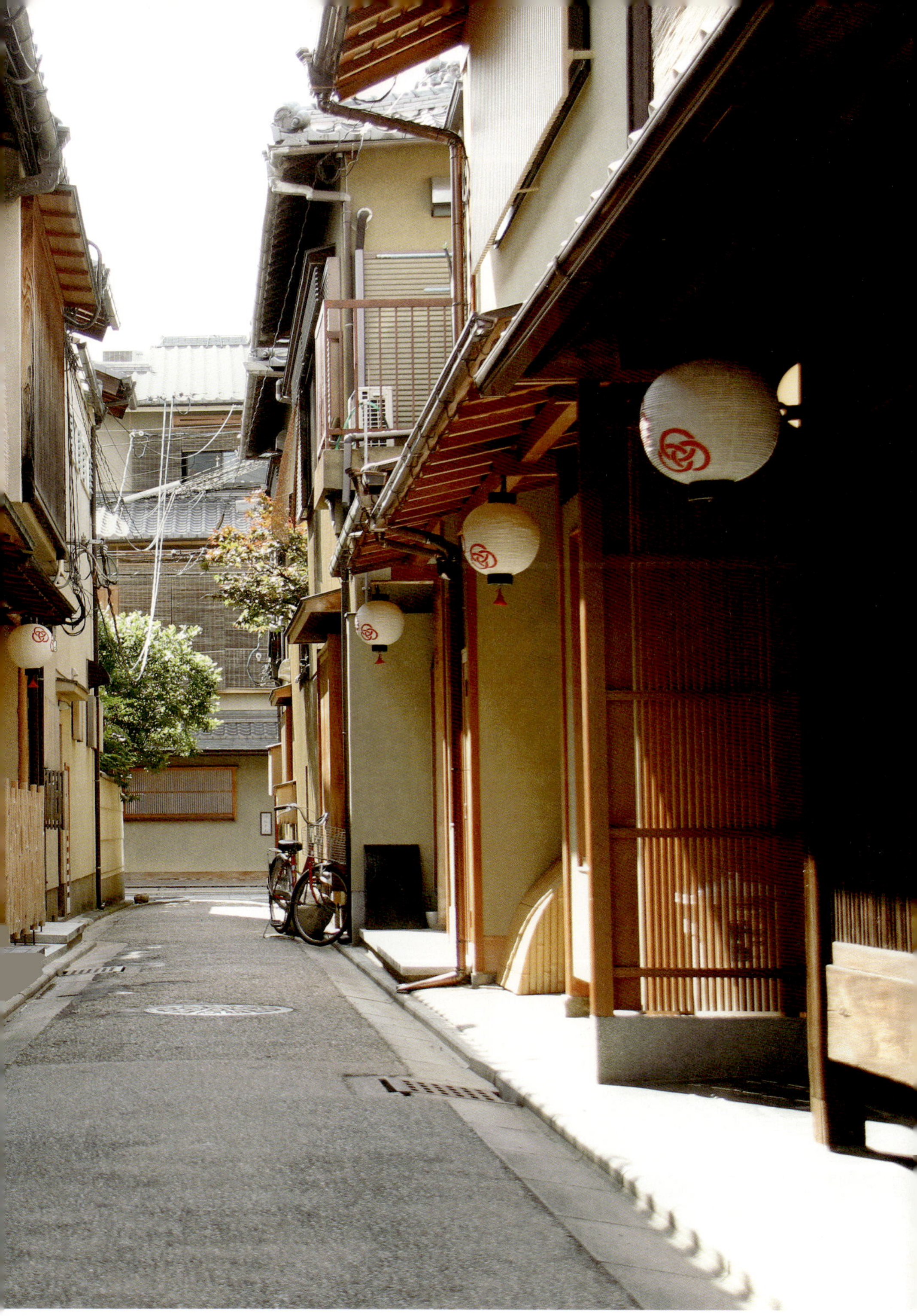

先斗町 | Pontocho

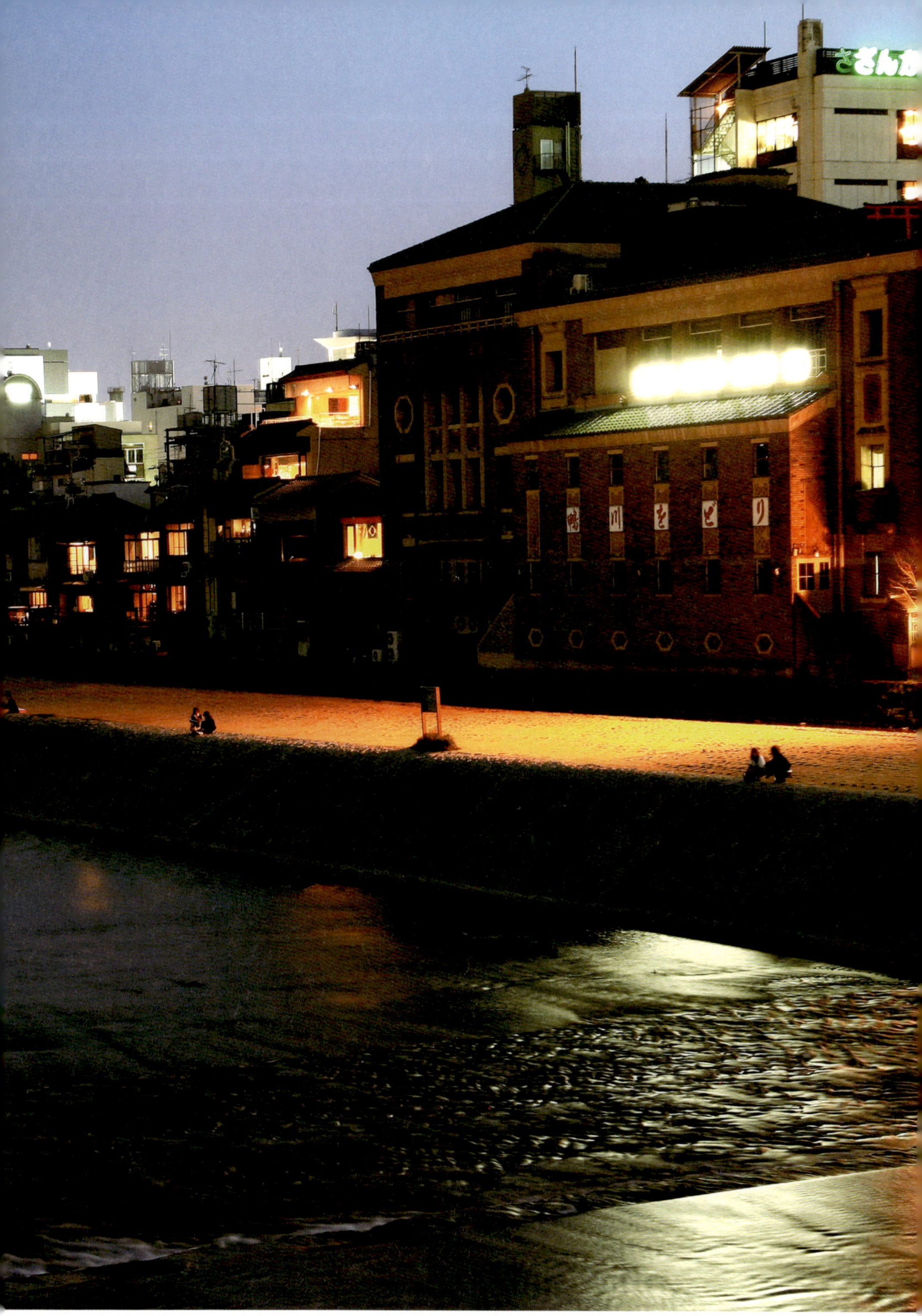
鴨川をどり

上七軒 | Kamishichiken

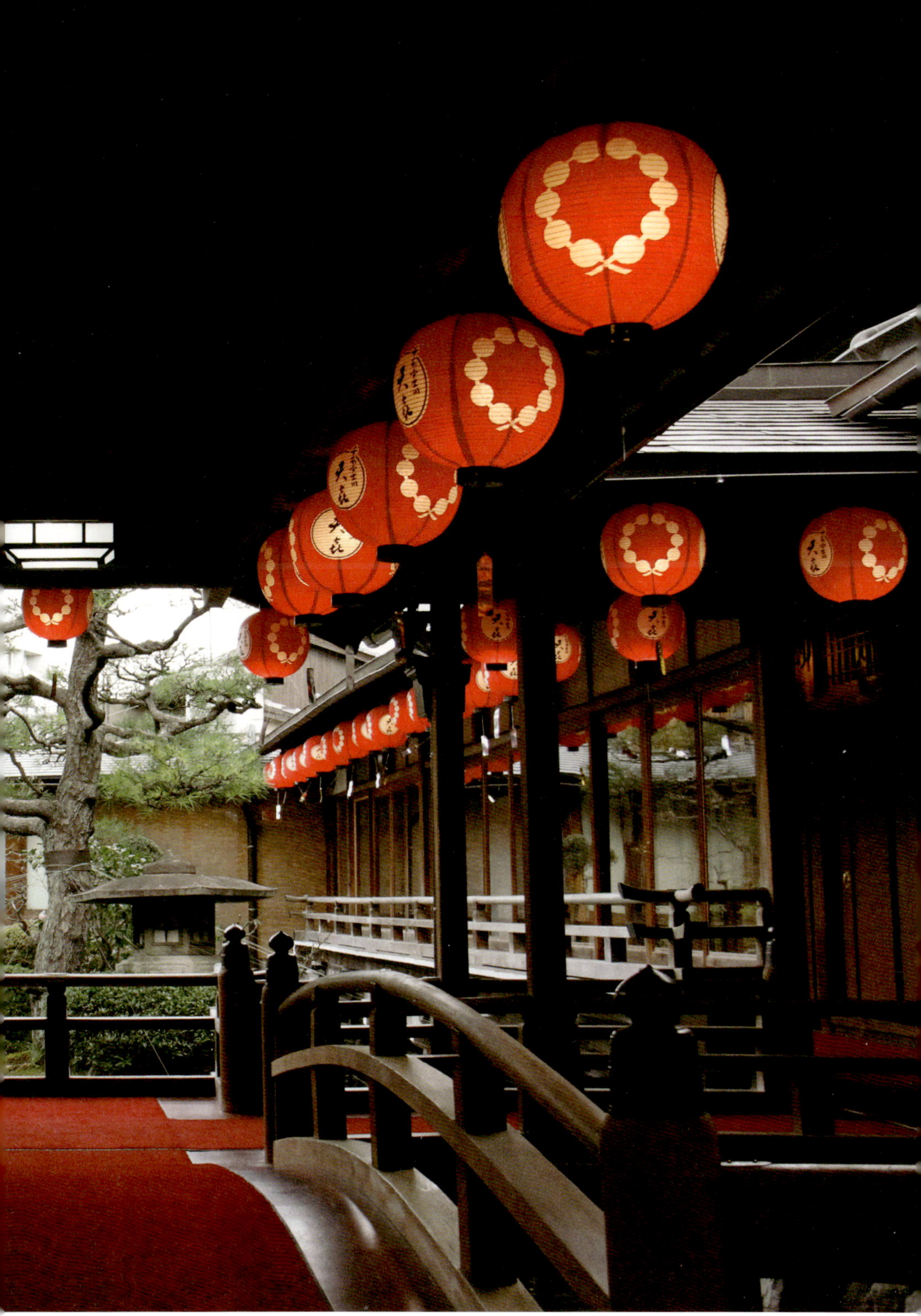

祇園東 | Gion Higashi

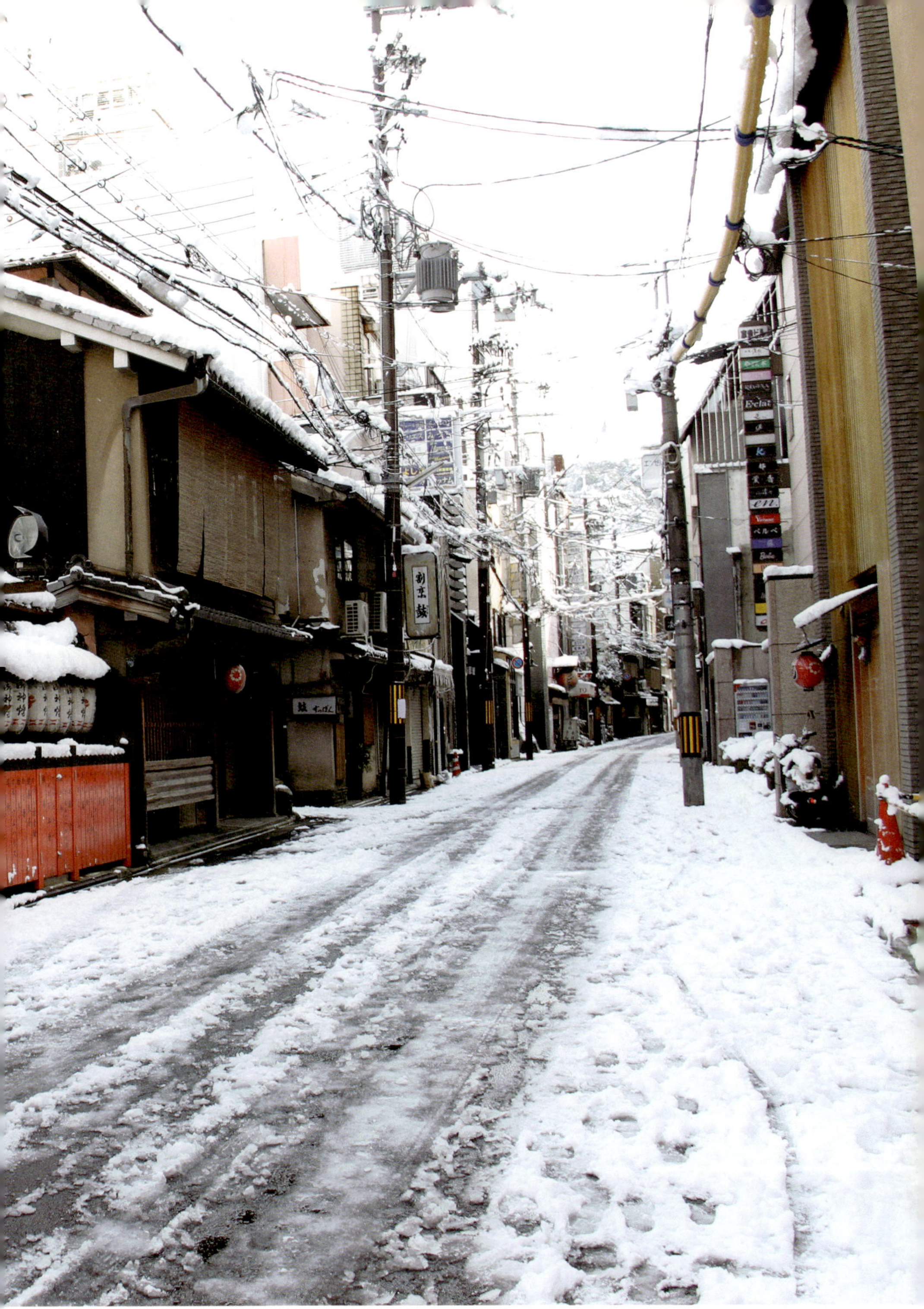
Eclat
en
ベルベ

京都の花街

　京の花街と聞いて、思い浮かべるのは何だろう。だらりの帯をしめ、おこぼをはいた舞妓、凛とした芸妓の舞姿、お茶屋の玄関に吊るされた提灯。どこからか聞こえる三味線、音楽のように交わされる京ことば、からからと格子戸が開く音。その魅力は、古今多くの人を捉え、絵画に描かれ、文学の題材ともなった。京都の花街を舞台とした映画も枚挙にいとまなく、古くは無声映画の時代にさかのぼる。金森万象監督の「祇園小唄絵日傘」(昭和5年)が大ヒットし、この映画に使われた「祇園小唄」(作詞：長田幹彦、作曲：佐々紅華)は全国に知られる歌となった。その後も様々な映画の舞台となり、近年では「舞妓Haaaan!!!」(平成19年　脚本：宮藤官九郎、監督：水田伸生)や、「舞妓はレディ」(平成26年　脚本・監督：周防正行)なども記憶に新しい。

　京都の祇園甲部、宮川町、先斗町、上七軒、祇園東の5つの花街を総称して五花街という。

　八坂神社門前の水茶屋に起源を持つ祇園(後に祇園甲部、祇園東に分かれる)、歌舞伎とのつながりの深い宮川町、北野天満宮門前の水茶屋に始まる上七軒、鴨川と高瀬川の間にあり、舟運の要所として栄えた先斗町と、それぞれの歴史、文化を持ち、今日までその伝統を伝えている。

　五花街の伝統的な町並を舞妓が行き交う光景は、京都の代表的なイメージのひとつといえるだろう。戦前は12歳位から舞妓になったが、現在は舞妓になるのは義務教育を終えてからである。舞妓になる前、仕込み・見習いの期間(半年～1年

間)に行儀作法や舞いなどを学び、舞妓としてデビュー(店出し)する。

　舞妓は屋方(置屋。屋形とも書く)に住む。一方、芸妓や舞妓たちが呼ばれる宴席となるお座敷があるのがお茶屋である。屋方の経営者やお茶屋の経営者は「おかあさん」と呼ばれ、年齢に拘わらず、先輩の舞妓や芸妓は「お姉さん」と呼ばれる。舞妓は舞などのお稽古に励み、平均して4〜5年ほどで芸妓になる(衿替え)。芸妓となっても日々芸を磨き、さらなる高みを目指しつづける。

　舞妓の花かんざしをはじめ、着物の柄、座敷のしつらいなど、花街は四季のうつろいを重んじる。始業式や八朔、事始めなど季節の節目ごとの行事も、しっかりと受け継がれている。また花街は祭との関わりも深い。八坂神社の氏子である祇園甲部、宮川町、先斗町、祇園東は祇園祭、北野天満宮の氏子である上七軒は梅花祭や瑞饋祭、五花街が交替で参加する時代祭などである。

　そしてなによりも華やかな行事が、春と秋のおどりや舞の舞台であろう。井上流の祇園甲部は「都をどり」と「温習会」、若柳流の宮川町は「京おどり」と「みずゑ会」、花柳流の上七軒は「北野をどり」と「寿会」、尾上流の先斗町は「鴨川をどり」と「水明会」、藤間流の祇園東は「祇園をどり」。芸妓、舞妓たちが日頃の鍛錬の成果を見せる舞台は、内外から広く支持されている。

　千年の都、京都。京の花街は歴史を彩り、幾多の物語が語りつがれ、そして今も新たな物語を紡ぎつづけている。

An Introduction to Kyoto's Kagai

Kagai, literally translated as "Flower Town," is the term Kyoto people use for the districts where the geiko and maiko practice the high-class arts that have made their beauty and refinement legendary the world over. There are five Kagai in Kyoto: Gion Kobu, Miyagawacho, Pontocho, Kamishichiken and Gion Higashi, which are known as Kyoto's Gokagai.

Each Kagai has its own unique historical origins and characteristics. The Gion district originally developed from the mizu-chaya (a kind of tea shop which served tea and light meals for visitors) in front of the gates leading to Yasaka Shrine. Gion later divided into two separate districts: Gion Kobu and Gion Higashi. Miyagawacho is strongly connected with the world of kabuki (traditional Japanese performing art form). Kamishichiken developed from the mizu-chaya in front of Kitano Tenmangu Shrine. Pontocho, which lies along a narrow lane next to the Kamo River, developed with the rising prosperity created by Takase Canal transportation artery.

Maiko, dressed up in darari obi (a long sash that hangs down at the back) and okobo (special high wooden clogs) are a universal image of all Kagai. Before World War 2, a maiko's training started around the age of twelve. Today, a maiko's education begins when she is about 16, after she has finished her compulsory education. In the year before officially becoming a maiko, she undergoes a period of training called Shikomi or Minarai when she studies classical Japanese manners, speech and other forms of etiquette. Then she begins her training to become a full-fledged geiko, usually over a four or five year period. Her debut as a geiko is called the Erikae (literally "changing of the collar"). Geiko are professional entertainers (especially in traditional dance and song and the use of traditional musical instruments) who constantly polish their skills through regular lessons with recognized teachers.

Maiko generally live in an establishment called a yakata or okiya, together with a woman called oka-san (lit. mother; the female manager of the establishment who takes care of everything). Geiko and maiko performances are staged in ozashiki (formal tatami mat rooms) at ochaya (a place where geiko and maiko entertain guests over dinner or during an event), which are also owned by female managers called oka-san. Upon the request of their clients, ochaya oka-san make the reservations or appointments with the requested number of geiko and maiko. The oka-san also arranges to provide the elaborate food and drink for the guests that will attend the evening's entertainment in the ozashiki. An evening can be a short, intimate meal or a longer large, boisterous party.

The yearly calendar of each Kagai revolves around seasonal changes, local history and local religious rituals and ceremonies. Some events are connected with important seasonal markers. Others function as a way of expressing gratitude to teachers or honoring great heroes of the past. Kagai are also intimately linked with local shrines and festivals. Gion Kobu, Miyagawacho, Pontocho and Gion Higashi have a strong connection with Yasaka Shrine and the Gion Festival (one of the three greatest festivals in Japan, held in July). Kamishichiken is affiliated with Kitano Tenmangu Shrine which hosts both the Plum Festival (in February) and Zuiki Festival (in October). Geiko and maiko from each Kagai join the annual Jidai Festival (one of Kyoto's three most important festivals held in October) on a rotating basis.

Kyoto's 1200 years of history are exquisitely expressed by the refined movement and beauty of geiko and maiko. Whether dance, literature, history or the changing seasons, you will find all this and more in the mysterious, sublime worlds of Kagai.

16

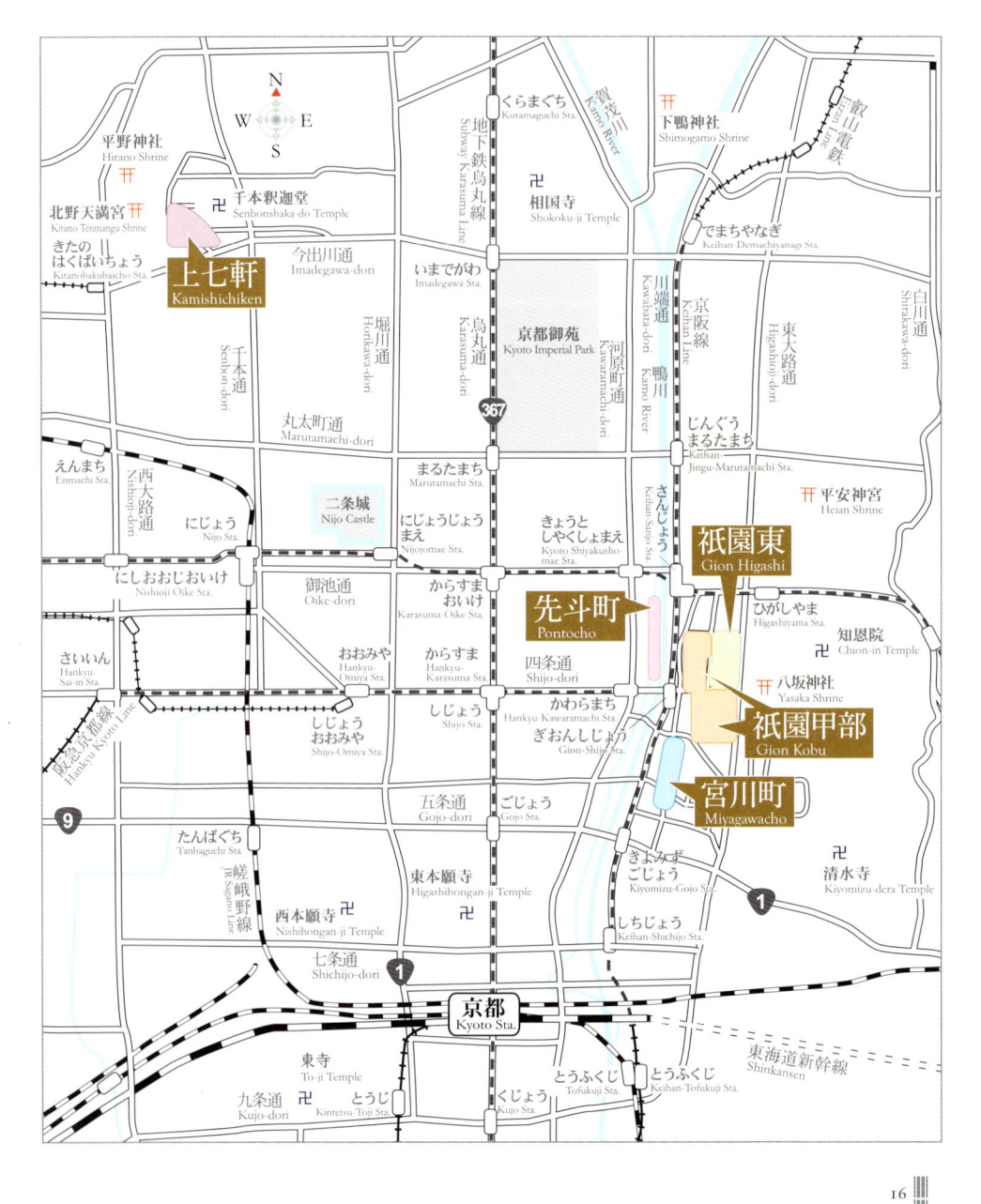

目次

京都の花街 ……………………………………………………………… 12
An Introduction to Kyoto's Kagai

第一章　芸妓・舞妓の美 ……………………………………………… 19
Chapter 1: Elegance of Geiko and Maiko

　　舞妓の髪型 ………………………………………………………… 44
　　Maiko Hairstyles

　　花かんざし ………………………………………………………… 70
　　Elaborate Flowery Ornaments

第二章　華やかなおどりの舞台 ……………………………………… 83
Chapter 2: Splendor of Dance Stage

第三章　花街の四季 …………………………………………………… 123
Chapter 3: Four Seasons in Kagai

第四章　昭和四十八〜昭和六十年の祇園 …………………………… 177
Chapter 4: Gion between 1973 and 1985

第五章　舞妓から芸妓へ―祇園甲部・紗月の5年間― ……… 225
Chapter 5: Transition from Maiko to Geiko – The 5 year record of Satsuki in Gion Kobu

　　店出し ……………………………………………………………… 230
　　Misedashi – Official Debut as a Maiko

　　衿替え ……………………………………………………………… 278
　　Erikae – Transition from a Maiko to Geiko

五花街紹介 ……………………………………………………………… 289
Introduction of the Gokagai

公益財団法人京都伝統伎芸振興財団（おおきに財団）の紹介 ……… 300

あとがき ………………………………………………………………… 301

表紙カバーの写真：店出し（祇園東）

〈凡例〉

開催日

行事名

行事が行われる花街名

十日ゑびす 残り福祭 | Toka Ebisu Festival

1月11日（祇園甲部・宮川町）

January 11 (Gion Kobu, Miyagawacho)

1月8日から12日まで京都恵美須神社にて行われる十日ゑびす。11日の残り福祭では舞妓による福餅と福笹の授与が行われる。

Toka Ebisu is a famous traditional festival in Kyoto held at Ebisu Shrine from January 8th to 12th. On the 11th, maiko distribute bamboo branches with auspicious decorations and rice cakes to visitors.

写真キャプション

写真の芸妓・舞妓などの花街を表します

福餅と福笹の授与 | Giving auspicious rice cakes and bamboo decorations to people

祇園甲部 | Gion Kobu

Elegance of Geiko and Maiko

第一章
Chapter 1

芸妓・舞妓の美

着付 | **Kimono Dressing**　先斗町 | Pontocho

店出し | Misedashi – Official debut as a maiko   先斗町 | Pontocho

店出し | Misedashi – Official debut as a maiko　祇園甲部 | Gion Kobu

だらりの帯 | Darari Obi – Maiko's elaborate long sash on the back　祇園甲部 | Gion Kobu

新年の挨拶 | New Year's Greetings　宮川町 | Miyagawacho

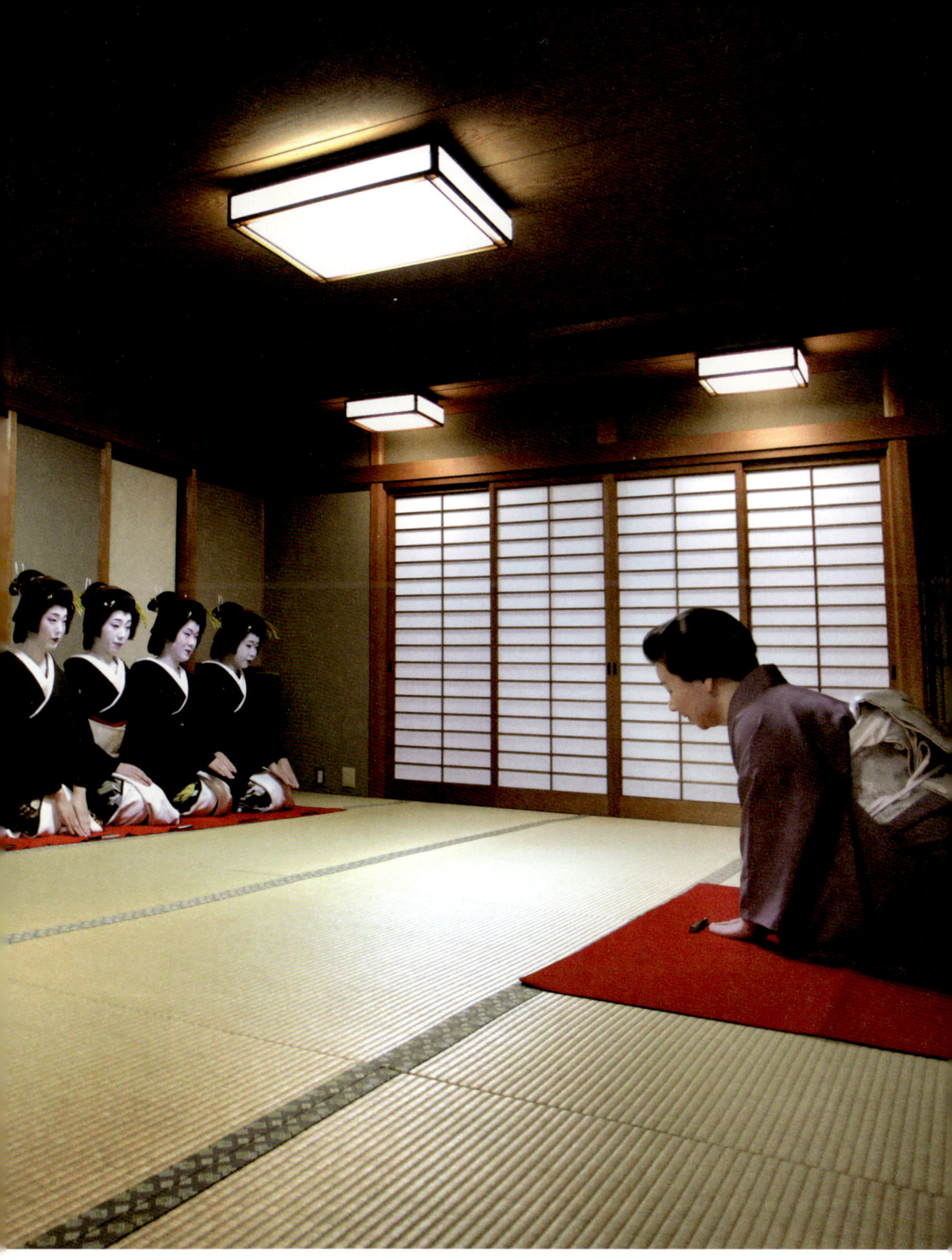

店出し | Misedashi – Official debut as a maiko　宮川町 | Miyagawacho

店出し | Misedashi – Official debut as a maiko　祇園甲部 | Gion Kobu

店出し | Misedashi – Official debut as a maiko　上七軒 | Kamishichiken

芸妓からの店出し | Misedashi as a geiko　上七軒 | Kamishichiken

店出し | Misedashi – Official debut as a maiko　祇園東 | Gion Higashi

店出し | Misedashi – Official debut as a maiko　　祇園東 | Gion Higashi

年始まわり | New Year's Greeting Visit　宮川町 | Miyagawacho

雪の朝 | A snowy morning　宮川町 | Miyagawacho

だらりの帯 | Darari Obi – Maiko's elaborate long sash on the back　上七軒 | Kamishichiken

稲穂のかんざし │ Hair ornament with a real rice stalk　　宮川町 │ Miyagawacho

始業式 | Shigyoshiki – Year Opening Ceremony　祇園甲部 | Gion Kobu

始業式 | Shigyoshiki – Year Opening Ceremony　　宮川町 | Miyagawacho

初寄り | Hatsuyori New Year Gathering　祇園甲部 | Gion Kobu

39

初寄り | Hatsuyori New Year Gathering　祇園甲部 | Gion Kobu

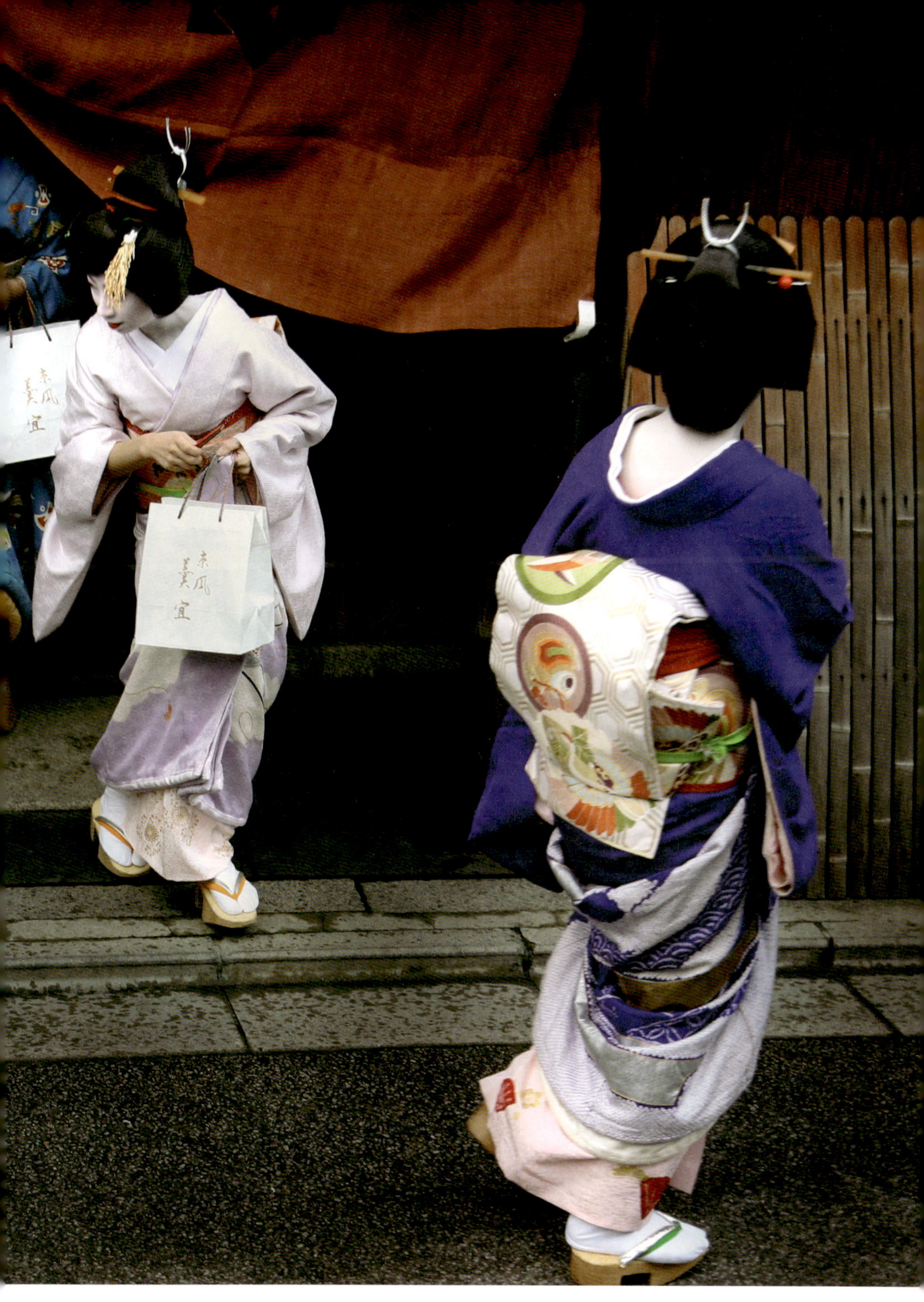

舞妓 | Maiko　先斗町 | Pontocho

舞妓 | Maiko　先斗町 | Pontocho

舞妓の髪型

舞妓になって初めて結うのが「割れしのぶ」。その後3年目ぐらいからは「おふく」となり、衿替えが近づくと「先笄」を結う。その他、「おふく」の舞妓が正装の時に結う「奴島田」や、祇園祭の時に結う「勝山」などがある。

割れしのぶ（正装用）｜ Ware Shinobu (for formal occasions)

店出しの3日間結う髪型。びら（銀の挿し物）を左右に挿す。

割れしのぶ｜ Ware Shinobu

舞妓の初期の髪型。店出ししてから2年位まで結う。

おふく｜ Ofuku

3年目位から結う髪型。赤い鹿の子が後ろだけ見えるようになる。かんざしも少し地味なものになる。

先笄｜ Sakko

衿替えの前2週間位結う髪型。結い上げた髪の「橋の毛」と呼ばれる部分の先を切るのが特徴。

Maiko Hairstyles

The very first hairstyle for a new maiko is called "Ware Shinobu." After a few years, they change the style to "Ofuku," and follow this by the one called "Sakko." Sakko is the style for a maiko whose "Erikae (transition from maiko to geiko)" is coming soon. A maiko with "Ofuku" style sets another style called "Yakko Shimada" for formal occasions. "Katsuyama" is the special hairstyle which is seen only during the Gion Festival time in July.

奴島田 | Yakko Shimada

普段「おふく」の舞妓が正月や八朔など正装の黒紋付を着る時に結う髪型。

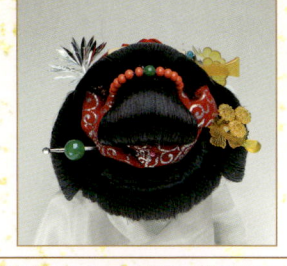

勝山 | Katsuyama

普段「おふく」の舞妓が祇園祭の頃結う髪型。「ぼん天」と呼ばれるなでしこの花をあしらった銀色のかんざしをつける。

先笄と「黒髪」| Sakko and "Kuro-kami" Dance – Preparation to be a geiko

衿替えを前に髪型は先笄に変わり、お歯黒をする場合もある。お座敷では「黒髪」を舞い、この時期しか見られない姿、舞の披露とあって、多くのお座敷に引っ張りだことなる。

Before the Erikae (transition from maiko to geiko), a maiko changes her hairstyle from Ofuku to Sakko and some paint her teeth in black (sign of a matured woman). She performs a dance titled "Kuro-kami (Black Hair)" in ozashiki.

「黒髪」を舞う | A maiko performing "Kuro-kami (Black Hair)"

お歯黒

Ohaguro – Painted teeth in black (a traditional sign of a matured woman)

化粧 | Makeup 先斗町 | Pontocho

鏡台 | Geiko in the mirror　祇園甲部 | Gion Kobu

芸妓 | Geiko　先斗町 | Pontocho

源光庵にて | At Genko-an Temple

舞妓 | Maiko　先斗町 | Pontocho

お茶屋の玄関にて | Entrance of ochaya　先斗町 | Pontocho

石畳と舞妓 | A maiko on the stone-paved street　先斗町 | Pontocho

だらりの帯 | Darari Obi – Maiko's elaborate long sash on the back　先斗町 | Pontocho

衿替えを前に「菊重ね」の髪型を結った舞妓 | A maiko with the hairstyle "Kiku-gasane" just before Erikae
先斗町 | Pontocho

舞妓 | Maiko　先斗町 | Pontocho

梅の花かんざし | Hair ornament of plum blossom design　祇園甲部 | Gion Kobu

都をどり お茶席 | Tea ceremony at Miyako Odori　祇園甲部 | Gion Kobu

北野をどり お茶席 | Tea ceremony at Kitano Odori　上七軒 | Kamishichiken

京おどり お茶席 | Tea ceremony at Kyo Odori　宮川町 | Miyagawacho

鴨川をどり　お茶席 | Tea ceremony at Kamogawa Odori　先斗町 | Pontocho

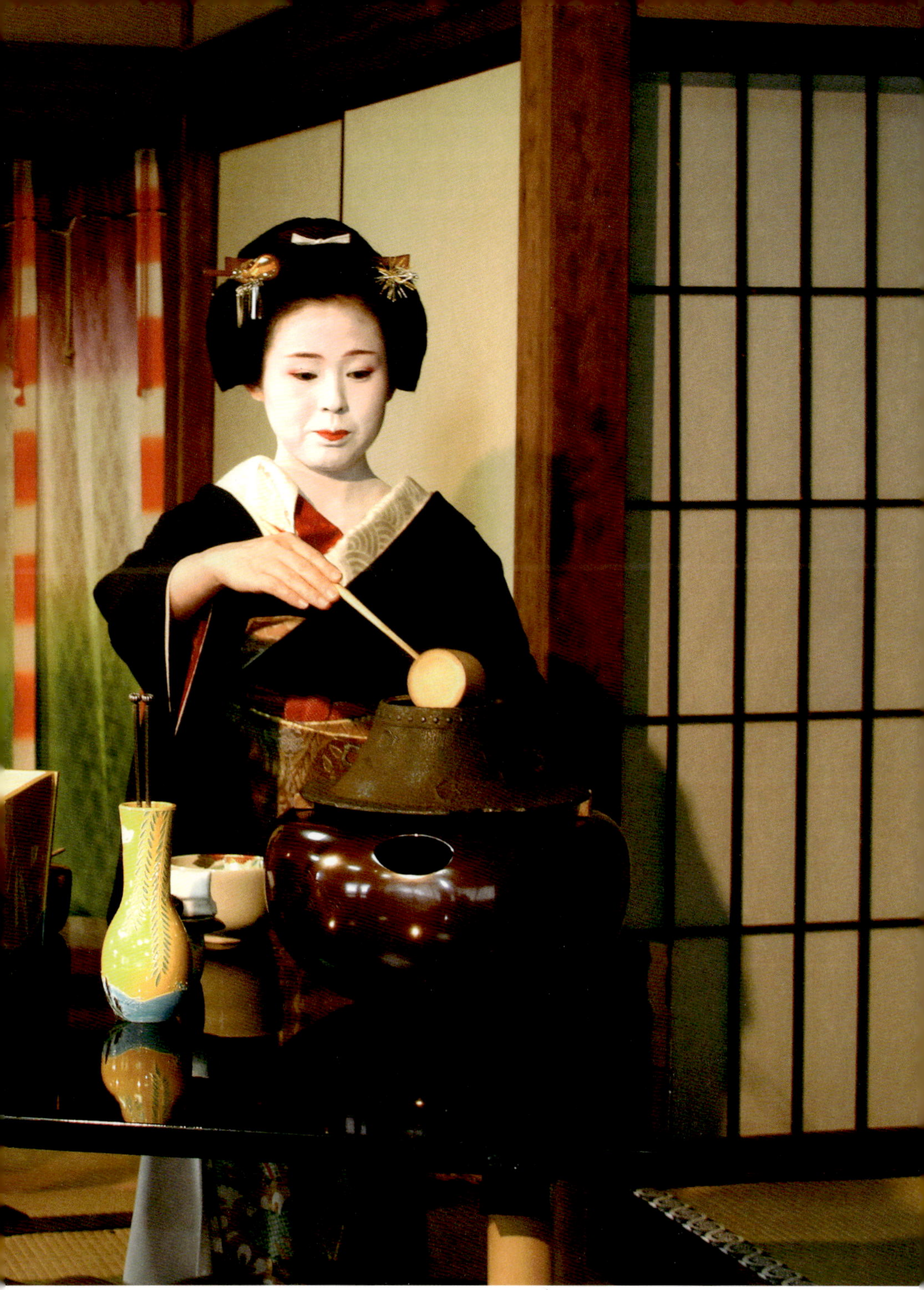

祇園をどり　お茶席 | Tea ceremony at Gion Odori　祇園東 | Gion Higashi

白い陽ざし | White sunbeam　祇園甲部 | Gion Kobu

八朔 | Hassaku Summer Greetings　　祇園甲部 | Gion Kobu

八朔 | Hassaku Summer Greetings　　祇園甲部 | Gion Kobu

店出し 着付け | Kimono dressing for Misedashi　先斗町 | Pontocho

店出し だらりの帯 | Misedashi – Back shot of a maiko with an elaborate long sash on her back

先斗町 | Pontocho

夏のよそおい | Summer attire　宮川町 | Miyagawacho

夏のよそおい | Summer attire　祇園甲部 | Gion Kobu

花かんざし

舞妓のさす華やかな花かんざし。月ごとにかわる四季折々のかんざしに加えて、祭の時のみ付ける特別なかんざしなどもある。正月には本物の稲穂に小さな白い鳩のついたかんざしも付ける。また12月の「まねき」には顔見世総見の際、お気に入りの役者にサインを入れてもらう。

1月 松竹梅
January: Pine, Bamboo, Plum

2月 梅
February: Plum Blossom

3月 菜の花
March: Nanohana (field mustard flower)

4月 桜
April: Cherry Blossom

5月 藤
May: Wisteria Flower

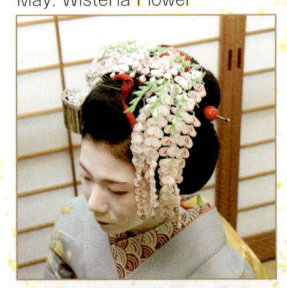

6月 柳
June: Willow Tree

70

Elaborate Flowery Ornaments

Elegant and colorful hair ornaments in a maiko's hair add even more gorgeousness to her beauty. They are called Hana Kanzashi and there are many designs depending on the month and seasonal events in Kyoto. Some are worn only for a very limited period of time, for example the ornament with real rice stalks and a little white pigeon decoration is worn only during the New Year's days.

7月 団扇
July: Uchiwa (round fan)

8月 薄
August: Japanese Silver Grass

9月 桔梗
September: Bell Flower

10月 菊
October: Chrysanthemum Flower

11月 もみじ
November: Maple Leaf

12月 まねき
December: Maneki (name signs of kabuki actors hung at the Minamiza Theatre)

71

鳴物のお稽古 | Lesson of Japanese hand drum　宮川町 | Miyagawacho

常磐津のお稽古 | Lesson of Tokiwazu traditional Japanese music　宮川町 | Miyagawacho

お座敷舞 | Dance performed in an ozashiki　　祇園甲部 | Gion Kobu

お座敷へ | Beginning of ozashiki 祇園甲部 | Gion Kobu

障子と舞妓 | Paper sliding door and a maiko　先斗町 | Pontocho

夏のお座敷 | Summer ozashiki　祇園甲部 | Gion Kobu

障子 | Maiko behind the paper sliding door

影 | Silhouette

初寄り | Hatsuyori New Year Gathering　祇園甲部 | Gion Kobu

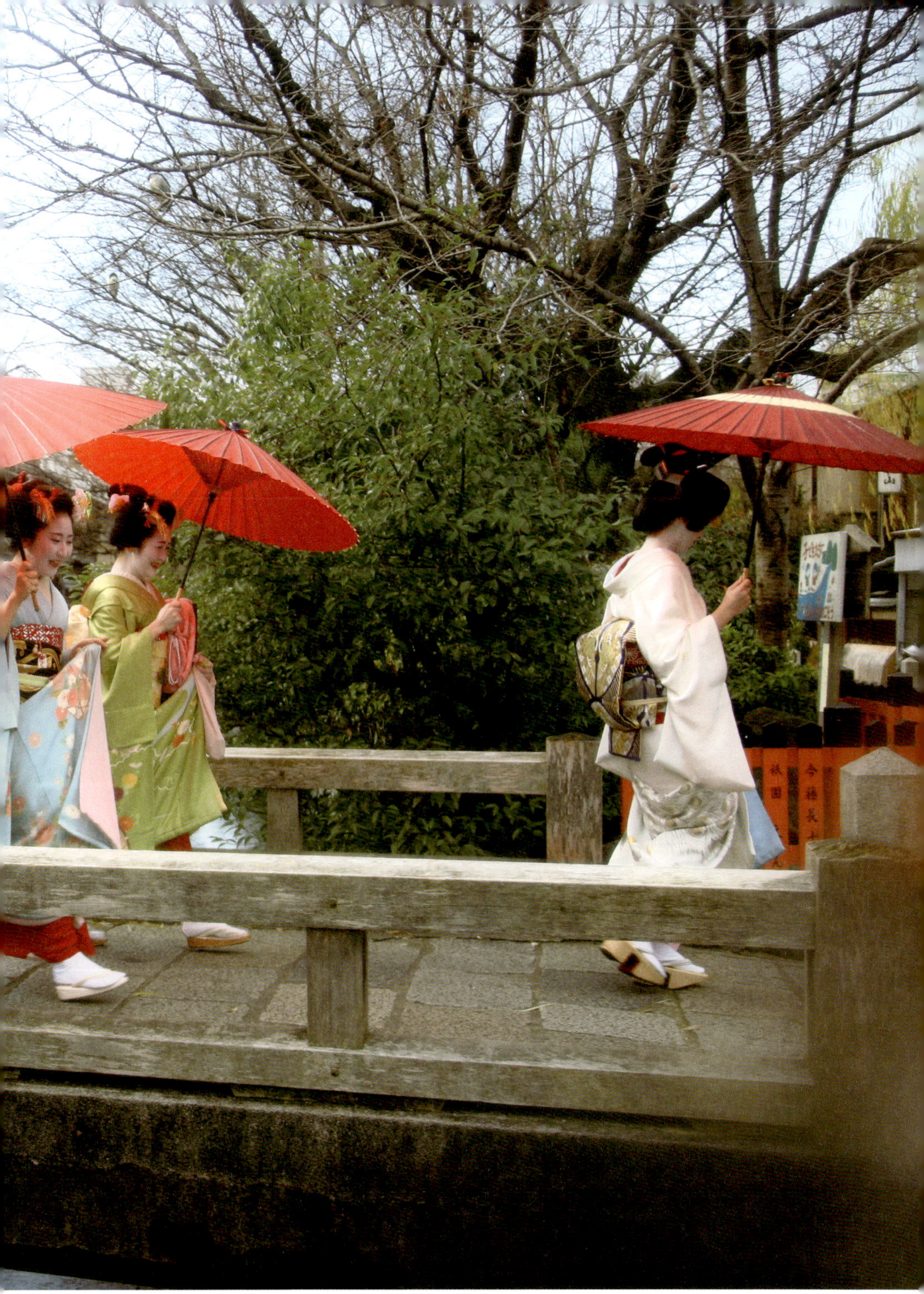

初寄り | Hatsuyori New Year Gathering　祇園甲部 | Gion Kobu

第二章

華やかな
おどりの舞台

Chapter 2

Splendor of Dance Stage

都をどり | Miyako Odori (Gion Kobu)

4月1日〜30日

祇園甲部の芸妓、舞妓たちの舞の舞台。「都をどりはヨーイヤサァー」のかけ声とともに華やかに幕が開く。明治5年(1872)、京都博覧会にて披露されたことに始まり、以来祇園甲部の舞は「京舞の井上流一本で」となった。

April 1-30

The Miyako Odori dance performed in the Inoue School style by the geiko and maiko of Gion Kobu. This exquisite traditional dance was first performed in 1872 when Kyoto hosted the National Expo. It has been one of Kyoto's best-loved and best-known spring events for over 140 years.

「平清盛由縁名所」(平成24年 第140回公演)より | The 140th Performance in 2012
祇園甲部 | Gion Kobu

「昔伝来大和宝尽」(平成26年 第142回公演)より | The 142nd Performance in 2014

祇園甲部 | Gion Kobu

「昔伝来大和宝尽」（平成26年 第142回公演）より ｜ The 142nd Performance in 2014
祇園甲部 ｜ Gion Kobu

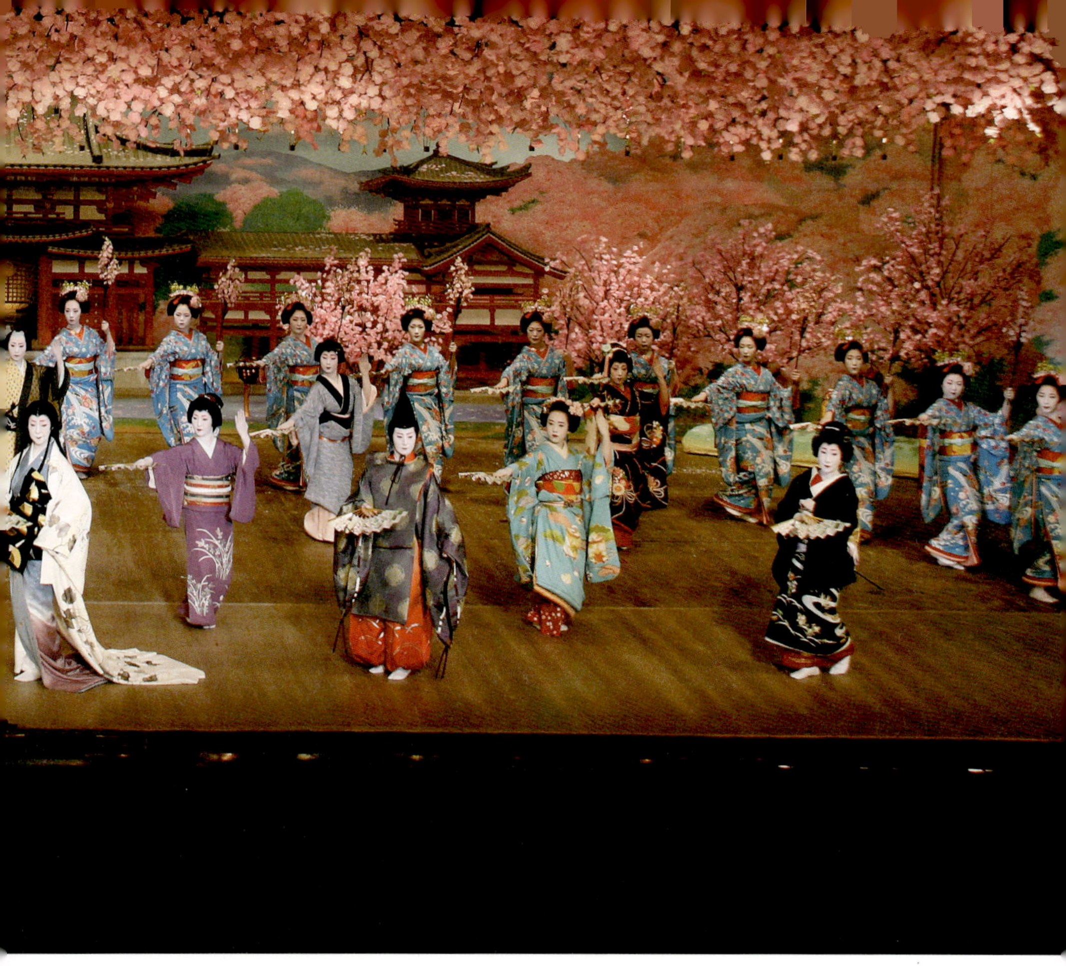

北野をどり | Kitano Odori (Kamishichiken)

3月25日〜4月7日

March 25-April 7

上七軒の芸妓、舞妓たちの舞の舞台。昭和27年（1952）、北野天満宮の千五十年大万燈会の際に芸を奉納したことに始まる。舞踊劇と純舞踊からなる華麗な舞台が観客を魅了し続けている。舞の流派は花柳流。

This traditional dance performance started in 1952 in Kamishichiken as a dedication for the 1050th anniversary of Kitano Tenmangu Shrine. The performance consists of dance drama and classical dances. Kamishichiken follows the dance style of the Hanayagi School.

「四條かぶき」（平成27年 第63回公演）より | The 63rd Performance in 2015
上七軒 | Kamishichiken

「上七軒夜曲」(平成27年 第63回公演)より | The 63rd Performance in 2015

上七軒 | Kamishichiken

「上七軒夜曲」(平成27年 第63回公演)より | The 63rd Performance in 2015　上七軒 | Kamishichiken

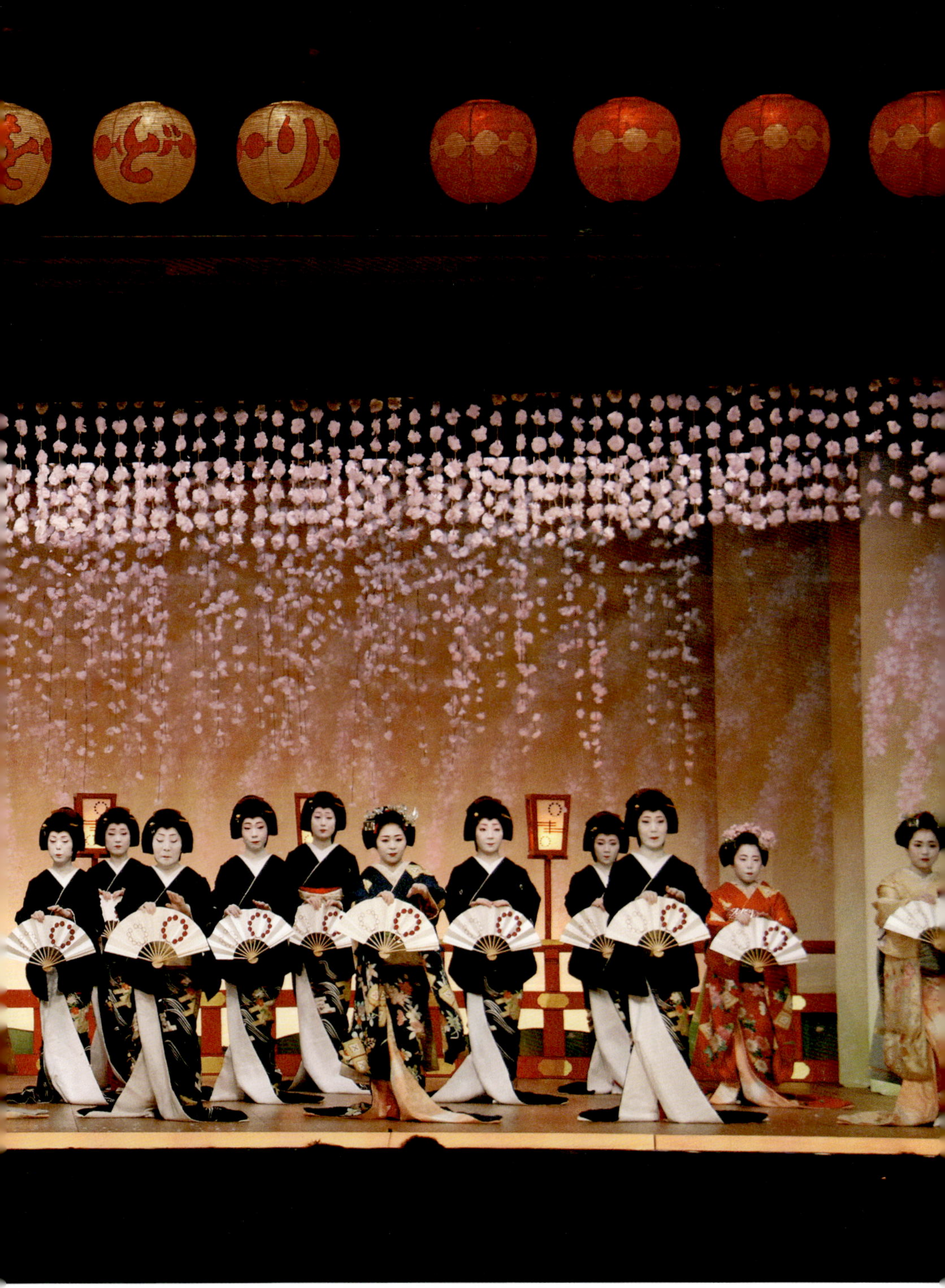
ど
り

京おどり | Kyo Odori (Miyagawacho)

4月第1土曜〜第3日曜 | First Saturday to third Sunday of April

宮川町の芸妓、舞妓たちの舞の舞台で、昭和25年(1950)に始まった。毎年趣向をこらした楽しい舞台が人気を呼んでいる。フィナーレ「宮川音頭」の芸妓、舞妓の総踊りは圧巻。舞の流派は若柳流。

This dance performance by the geiko and maiko of Miyagawacho started in 1950. The gorgeous finale, the Miyagawa Ondo, featuring all the geiko and maiko on stage together, always enchants the audience. Miyagawacho follows the dance style of the Wakayagi School.

「花都名所類聚」(平成20年 第59回公演)より | The 59th Performance in 2008
宮川町 | Miyagawacho

「雪月花雪暦」（平成26年 第65回公演）より ｜ The 65th Performance in 2014

宮川町 ｜ Miyagawacho

「雪月花雪暦」(平成26年 第65回公演)より「宮川音頭」 | The 65th Performance in 2014
宮川町 | Miyagawacho

95

鴨川をどり | Kamogawa Odori (Pontocho)

5月1日〜24日

初演は明治5年(1872)。昭和26年(1951)から平成10年(1998)までは年に2回、春と秋の興行があった。上演回数は平成27年で178回を数える。台詞の入ったいわゆる舞踊劇を特徴とする。流派は尾上流。

May 1-24

The first performance of this dance tradition was staged in 1872. Performances were held twice a year in spring and autumn from 1951 to 1998, and 2015 marks their 178th stage. Geiko and maiko perform the dance drama (with dialogue). Pontocho follows the dance style of the Onoe School.

「鏡山藤花繪」(平成26年 第177回公演)より | The 177th Performance in 2014

先斗町 | Pontocho

「鏡山藤花繪」(平成26年 第177回公演) より │ The 177th Performance in 2014　先斗町 │ Pontocho

「鏡山藤花繪」(平成26年 第177回公演) より | The 177th Performance in 2014　先斗町 | Pontocho

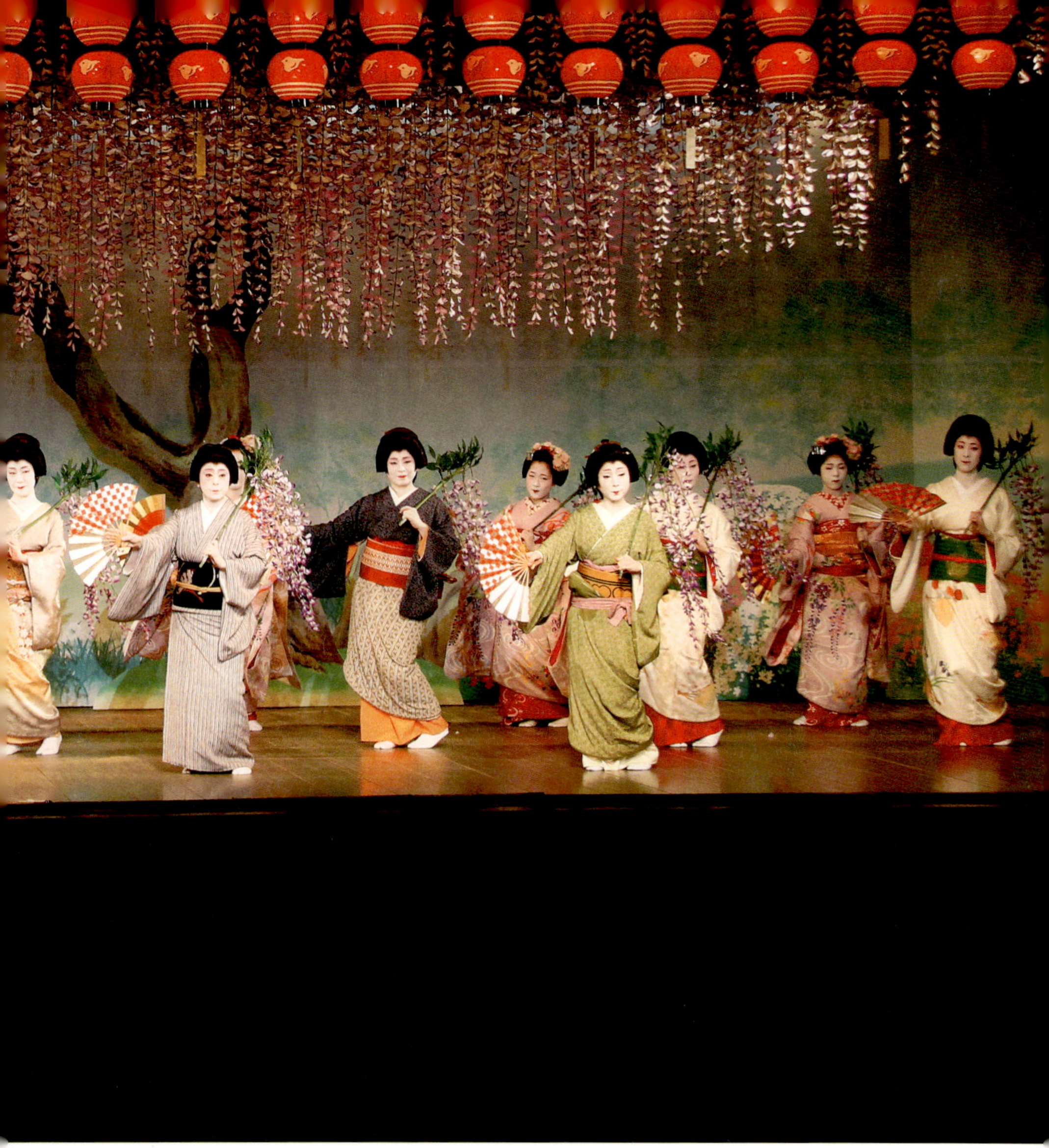

祇園をどり | Gion Odori (Gion Higashi)

11月1日〜10日

他の花街とは異なり、祇園東では秋に踊りの舞台が行われる。初演は昭和27年(1952)で流派は藤間流。フィナーレ「祇園東小唄」での芸妓、舞妓たちの総踊りは華やかさもひとしお。

November 1-10

The other four kagai hold similar dance performances in spring while Gion Higashi holds it in autumn. From the first performance in 1952, this annual dance, particularly the grand finale, "Gion Higashi Kouta," has always been an eagerly anticipated autumn event. Gion Higashi follows the dance style of the Fujima School.

「濃彩京襖絵」(平成26年 第57回公演)より | The 57th Performance in 2014　祇園東 | Gion Higashi

「濃彩京襖絵」(平成26年 第57回公演)より | The 57th Performance in 2014　祇園東 | Gion Higashi

「濃彩京襖絵」(平成26年 第57回公演)より | The 57th Performance in 2014　祇園東 | Gion Higashi

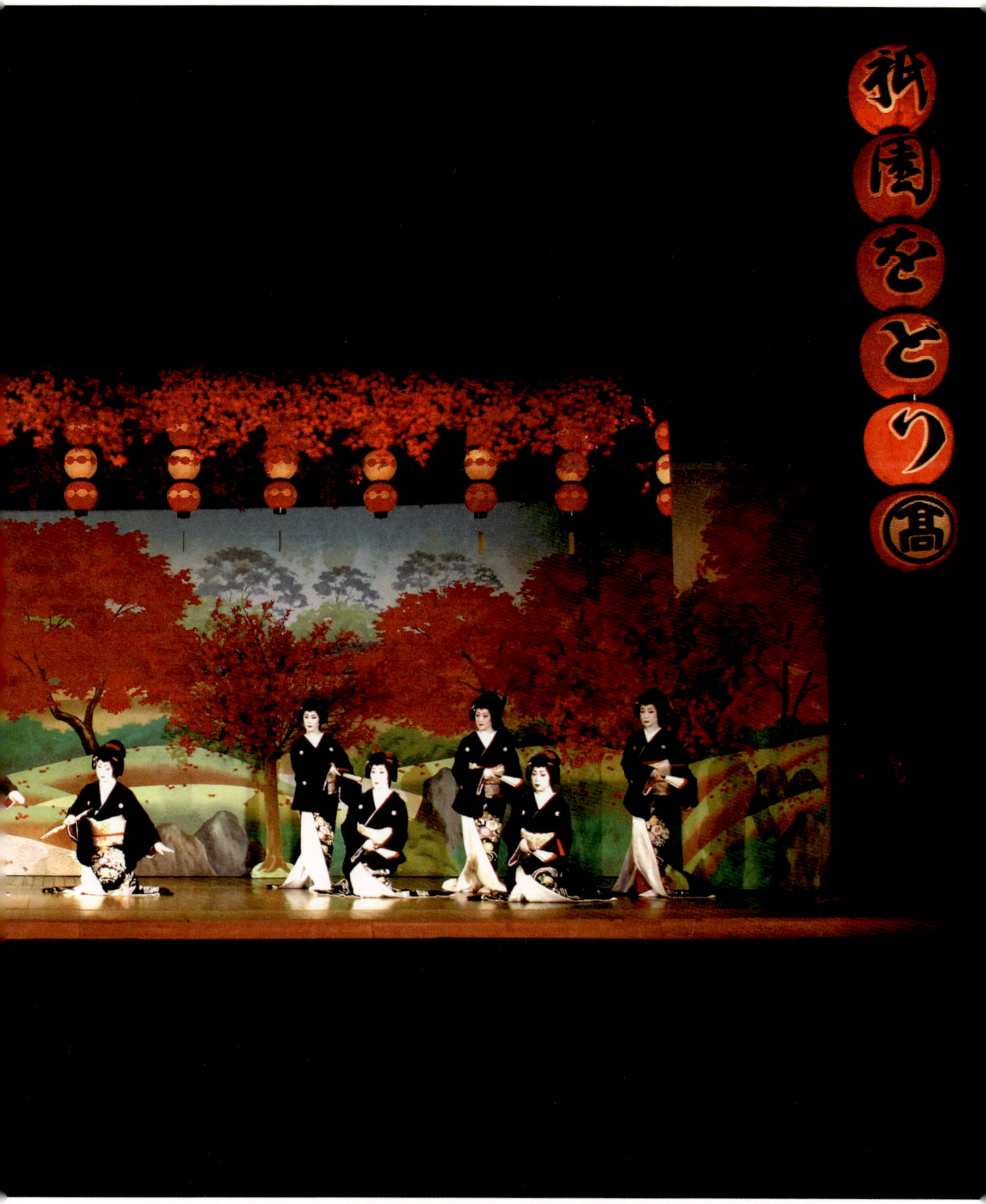
祇園をどり
髙

温習会 | Onshu-kai (Gion Kobu)

10月1日〜6日

祇園甲部、「京舞井上流」の秋の舞の発表会。明治初期に始まり、当初は毎月の開催であったとも伝わるが、詳細は不明。通好みの舞台でひいき客が多い。

October 1-6

This is an annual autumn dance performance of Gion Kobu following the dance style of the Inoue School that started in the early Meiji period (late 19th century). The elaborate dances continue to attract long-term fans.

「木賀の宿」(平成23年公演)より | Performance in 2011　祇園甲部 | Gion Kobu

「梓」(平成23年公演)より | Performance in 2011　祇園甲部 | Gion Kobu

みずゑ会 | Mizue-kai (Miyagawacho)

10月上旬

Early October

平成18年(2006)に35年振りに復活した宮川町の秋の踊りの発表会。日頃の精進の成果が披露され、最後は「宮川小唄」の総踊りで締めくくられる。

After a 35-year hiatus, this autumn dance performance by geiko and maiko in Miyagawacho was revived in 2006. A song "Miyagawa Kouta" makes for a gorgeous finale.

「助六」(平成25年公演)より | Performance in 2013　宮川町 | Miyagawacho

「宮川小唄」(平成25年公演)より | Performance in 2013　宮川町 | Miyagawacho

「乗合船恵方万歳」(平成25年公演)より | Performance in 2013　上七軒 | Kamishichiken

寿会 | Kotobuki-kai (Kamishichiken)

10月中旬頃

上七軒の秋の舞の発表会。古典ものの踊りが中心で、春の「北野をどり」と趣を変えている。

Mid-October

Kotobuki-kai is an annual autumn dance performance in Kamishichiken. It features different types of classical dance pieces selected from the spring Kitano Odori performance.

水明会 | Suimei-kai (Pontocho)

10月中旬

先斗町の秋の舞踊の発表会。昭和5年(1930)から続けられ、平成25年(2013)には第100回を迎えた。

Mid-October

This is an annual autumn dance performance by geiko in Pontocho. It has been performed continually since 1930 and celebrated its 100th stage in 2013.

「金谷丹前」(平成22年公演)より | Performance in 2010　先斗町 | Pontocho

「熊野」(平成22年公演)より | Performance in 2010　先斗町 | Pontocho

「舞妓の賑い 祇園小唄」(平成25年第20回記念公演) より | The 20th Commemorative Performance in 2013

五花街 | Gion Kobu, Miyagawacho, Pontocho, Kamishichiken, Gion Higashi

都の賑い (京都五花街合同公演) | "Miyako no Nigiwai" Kyoto Gokagai Traditional Dance Performance

6月下旬
(祇園甲部・宮川町・先斗町・上七軒・祇園東)

Late June
(Gion Kobu, Miyagawacho, Pontocho, Kamishichiken, Gion Higashi)

五花街の芸妓、舞妓がそれぞれの花街の流儀で華麗な舞を披露する合同公演。平成6年(1994)に始まった。五花街から選りすぐられた芸妓、舞妓が日頃の稽古の成果を披露する。

This yearly event, started in 1994, is a graceful joint performance by geiko and maiko from all five Kagai. Geiko and maiko from each Kagai perform their own style of dances with pride.

「祇園手打 七福神・花づくし」(平成25年第20回記念公演)より　　祇園甲部 | Gion Kobu
The 20th Commemorative Performance in 2013

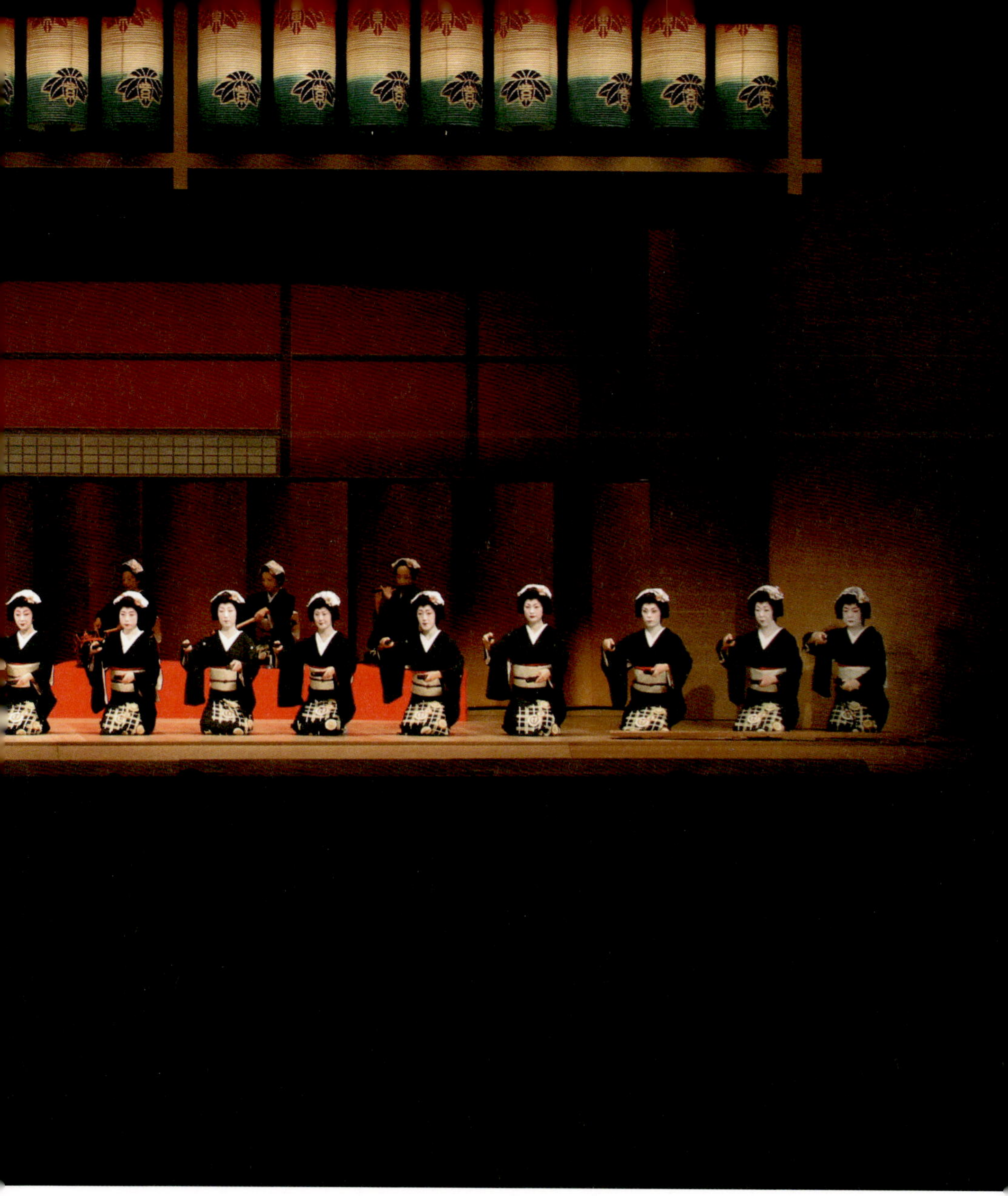

舞扇（鴨川をどり）より ｜ Folding fan for dancing (from Kamogawa Odori)　先斗町 ｜ Pontocho

舞台の情景(祇園をどり)より | A stage scene (from Gion Odori)　祇園東 | Gion Higashi

衣装合わせ | Costume Coordination

舞台の1カ月以上前に衣装合わせが行われ、ポスターやパンフレットに使われる写真撮影なども行われる。

Costume coordination preparation begins more than one month before the performance. Pictures for posters and brochures are also taken at this time.

京おどりの衣装合わせ | Costume coordination for Kyo Odori　宮川町 | Miyagawacho

大ざらえ | Ozarae

本番間近に行われる最終の舞台稽古。細部に至る厳しい指導のもと、総仕上げが行われる。

Ozarae is the final rehearsal before the show starts. Teachers give strict coaching in every detail.

京おどりの大ざらえ | Final rehearsal for Kyo Odori　　宮川町 | Miyagawacho

舞の輪 | Rings of Dance

120

121

夢舞い | Dance of Dream

第三章 Chapter 3

花街の四季

Four Seasons
in Kagai

お正月 祇園甲部の雪景色 | Snowy New Year's Day in Gion Kobu

始業式 | Shigyoshiki

1月7日（祇園甲部・宮川町・先斗町・祇園東）／
1月9日（上七軒）

January 7 (Gion Kobu, Miyagawacho, Pontocho, Gion Higashi)
January 9 (Kamishichiken)

前年の売り上げ成績のよいお茶屋、芸妓、舞妓を表彰し、新年にふさわしい舞が披露される。

In each Kagai, geiko and maiko attend the Shigyoshiki (year opening ceremony) in fully formal black kimono. During the ceremony, the most successful ochaya and individual geiko and maiko of the previous year for each district is presented with an award of excellence. New Year dance performances are also staged.

始業式で「倭文（やまとぶみ）」を舞う京舞井上流五世家元井上八千代
The 5th Yachiyo Inoue, the master of Inoue School of dance, who is performing "Yamatobumi" in the Shigyoshiki (year opening ceremony)

祇園甲部 | Gion Kobu

始業式で表彰を受ける芸舞妓たち | Maiko and geiko receiving the award　宮川町 | Miyagawacho

127

黒紋付に稲穂のかんざしが映える | Black kimono and hair ornament with real rice stalk – Very formal attire
宮川町 | Miyagawacho

始業式 客席から | A view of Shigyoshiki (year opening ceremony) from audience seat

上七軒 | Kamishichiken

年始の挨拶 | New Year's Greetings　先斗町 | Pontocho

十日ゑびす 残り福祭 | Toka Ebisu Festival

1月11日（祇園甲部・宮川町）

January 11 (Gion Kobu, Miyagawacho)

　1月8日から12日まで京都恵美須神社にて行われる十日ゑびす。11日の残り福祭では舞妓による福笹と福餅の授与が行われる。

Toka Ebisu is a famous traditional festival in Kyoto held at Ebisu Shrine from January 8th to 12th. On the 11th, maiko distribute bamboo branches with auspicious decorations and rice cakes to visitors.

福餅と福笹の授与 | Giving auspicious rice cakes and bamboo decorations to people
祇園甲部 | Gion Kobu

節分・お化け | Setsubun & Obake Disguise

2月2日・3日
（祇園甲部・宮川町・先斗町・上七軒・祇園東）

祇園甲部、宮川町、先斗町、祇園東は八坂神社、上七軒は北野天満宮にて、芸妓、舞妓による奉納舞と豆まきが行われる。また夕方以降は様々な装いに扮した芸妓、舞妓たちがお茶屋のお座敷をまわる「お化け」が行われる。

February 2, 3 (Gion Kobu, Miyagawacho, Pontocho, Kamishichiken, Gion Higashi)

Setsubun is a seasonal transition ritual held on the event of the New Year according to the old Chinese lunar calendar. Geiko and maiko perform a special dance for the deity and scatter dried soybeans to pray for good fortune. In the evening, maiko and geiko put on disguises and visit ochaya. This is called Obake and is a night filled with laughter, drinking and general fun.

八坂神社での豆まき | Bean scattering ceremony at Yasaka Shrine　祇園東 | Gion Higashi

お化け「二人阿古屋」八坂神社にて | Obake (disguise) "Futari Akoya" at Yasaka Shrine

宮川町 | Miyagawacho

お化け「禿のお遊び」 | Obake (disguise) "Kamuro no Oasobi"　先斗町 | Pontocho

お化け「三番叟」 | Obake (disguise) "Sanbaso"　祇園東 | Gion Higashi

梅花祭 | Plum Blossom Festival

2月25日(上七軒)

北野天満宮で行われる。菅原道真公の祥月命日にあたり、梅を愛でたという故事にちなみ、梅花の小枝を挿した「紙立」を供える。上七軒の芸妓、舞妓たちによる野点茶会も行われ、梅の咲き誇る境内は華やかな雰囲気につつまれる。

February 25 (Kamishichiken)

This is the memorial day for Michizane Sugawara, a famous scholar and politician of the 9th century, who is the deity enshrined at Kitano Tenmangu Shrine and loved plum blossoms deeply. An outdoor tea ceremony is hosted by geiko and maiko from the Kamishichiken.

梅花祭の野点茶会 | Open-air tea ceremony performed at the Plum Festival　上七軒 | Kamishichiken

祇園白川桜 ライトアップイベント | Night-time Cherry Blossom Lit Up Event in Gion Shirakawa

3月末頃(祇園東)

毎年、祇園白川桜ライトアップイベントでは様々な企画が行われ、平成26年(2014)は祇園東の舞妓によるお茶会が観亀稲荷神社にて行われた。

End of March (Gion Higashi)

Maiko from Gion Higashi performed tea ceremony and welcomed visitors. This was a part of special evening light-up event held during the cherry blossom season in 2014.

観亀稲荷神社の境内にて | At Kanki Inari Shrine　祇園東 | Gion Higashi

祇園白川 | Gion Shirakawa　祇園甲部 | Gion Kobu

平安神宮例大祭奉納舞踊 | Dance Dedication for Annual Festival of Heian Shrine

4月16日（祇園甲部・宮川町・先斗町・祇園東）

April 16 (Gion Kobu, Miyagawacho, Pontocho, Gion Higashi)

　4月15日は平安神宮の例祭。翌16日には、大極殿前の仮設舞台にて奉納行事が行われ、花街の奉納舞や、平安雅楽会の神楽、舞楽などが続く。

On April 15th, ceremonial events are held at Heian Shrine. The next day, dances by geiko and maiko are performed on a prominent stage in front of the shrine's vermilion Daigokuden ceremonial hall along with ancient court music and dances.

奉納舞 | Dance dedicated for the deity　　祇園甲部 | Gion Kobu

139

観亀稲荷神社例祭 | Kanki Inari Shrine Annual Festival

5月中旬（祇園東）

祇園東地区の防火や商売繁盛の神社として崇敬される観亀稲荷神社の例祭。

Mid-May (Gion Higashi)

The annual ceremonial event at Kanki Inari Shrine. The deity of this shrine is worshipped for protection from fire and business luck.

宵宮祭 | Yoi-miya Festival　祇園東 | Gion Higashi

例祭 | Rei-sai Festival　祇園東 | Gion Higashi

初夏の祇園白川 | Shirakawa Stream in summer

みやび会 | Miyabi-kai

7月初旬（祇園甲部）

井上八千代師とともに芸妓、舞妓が八坂神社に詣で、芸の上達と健康、京舞・井上流の門下生でつくる「みやび会」の発展を祈願する。毎年新調する揃いの浴衣姿が夏らしい。

Early July (Gion Kobu)

In this annual event of the Miyabi-kai, the name of the group that studies the dance style of the Inoue School, geiko and maiko visit Yasaka Shrine with Yachiyo Inoue, the master of the school, and pray for dance skills and the prosperity of their group. Every year, they make a new yukata summer kimono design.

井上八千代師とともに記念撮影
Photo session with the 5th Yachiyo Inoue, the master of Inoue School of dance
祇園甲部 | Gion Kobu

団扇　宮川町にて　| Round fans with names of geiko and maiko of Miyagawacho

祇園祭 | Gion Festival

7月1日～31日（祇園甲部・宮川町・先斗町・祇園東）

祇園祭は八坂神社のお祭で、平安初期に疫病の退散を祈願して矛をたてたことに始まるとされる。クライマックスは「コンチキチン」の祇園囃子を奏でながらの山鉾巡行だが、その前後1ヵ月にわたって様々な行事が行われる。祇園甲部、宮川町、先斗町、祇園東の各花街は花傘巡行や奉納舞などに参加する。

July 1-31 (Gion Kobu, Miyagawacho, Pontocho, Gion Higashi)

Ranked as one of Japan's top three festivals, the Gion Festival is an annual festival dedicated for Yasaka Shrine. The festival dates back to the early Heian period (794-1185) when a series of plagues were raging throughout the country. The climax of the festival is a procession of richly decorated wooden floats with Gion Bayashi festival music. Many other ceremonies and rituals are held throughout the month. Geiko and maiko of the Gion Kobu, Miyagawacho, Pontocho, and Gion Higashi districts participate in several events during the month-long festival.

宮川町を行く綾傘鉾の日和神楽
Hiyori Kagura Procession of Ayagasa-hoko Float going through Miyagawacho

神幸祭で花見小路を行く神輿
Mikoshi portable shrine procession of Shinko-sai Festival going through Hanamikoji Street

花傘巡行 | Hanagasa Junko Procession 先斗町 | Pontocho

奉納舞「コンチキ踊」| Dance dedicated for the deity of Yasaka Shrine　宮川町 | Miyagawacho

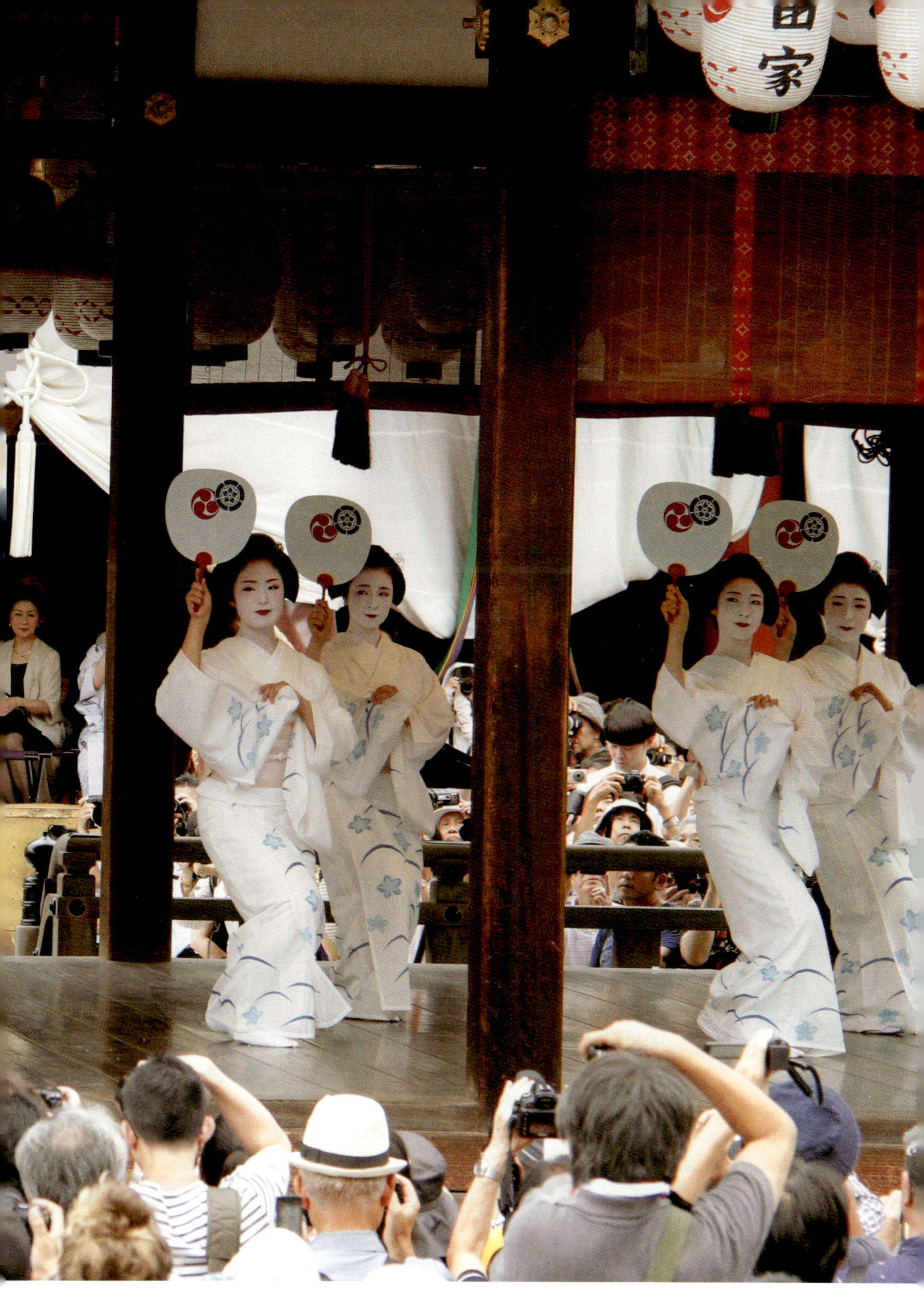
家

八朔 | Hassaku

8月1日（祇園甲部・宮川町・先斗町・上七軒・祇園東）

八朔とは8月1日の意。日頃お世話になっているお師匠さんやお茶屋さんなどをまわり、感謝をこめて「おめでとうさんどす」と挨拶をする。

August 1 (Gion Kobu, Miyagawacho, Pontocho, Kamishichiken, Gion Higashi)

Hassaku is a name of August 1st. On this day, geiko and maiko pay their respects to their teachers and the various ochaya they are indebted to. Gratitude is expressed in the Kyoto dialect with: "Omedetosan-dosu." This is a traditional mid-summer event in Kagai.

八朔 | Hassaku Summer Greetings　　先斗町 | Pontocho

八朔 | Hassaku Summer Greetings　祇園甲部 | Gion Kobu

芙蓉と上七軒の路地 | Mallow rose flowers on a street in Kamishichiken

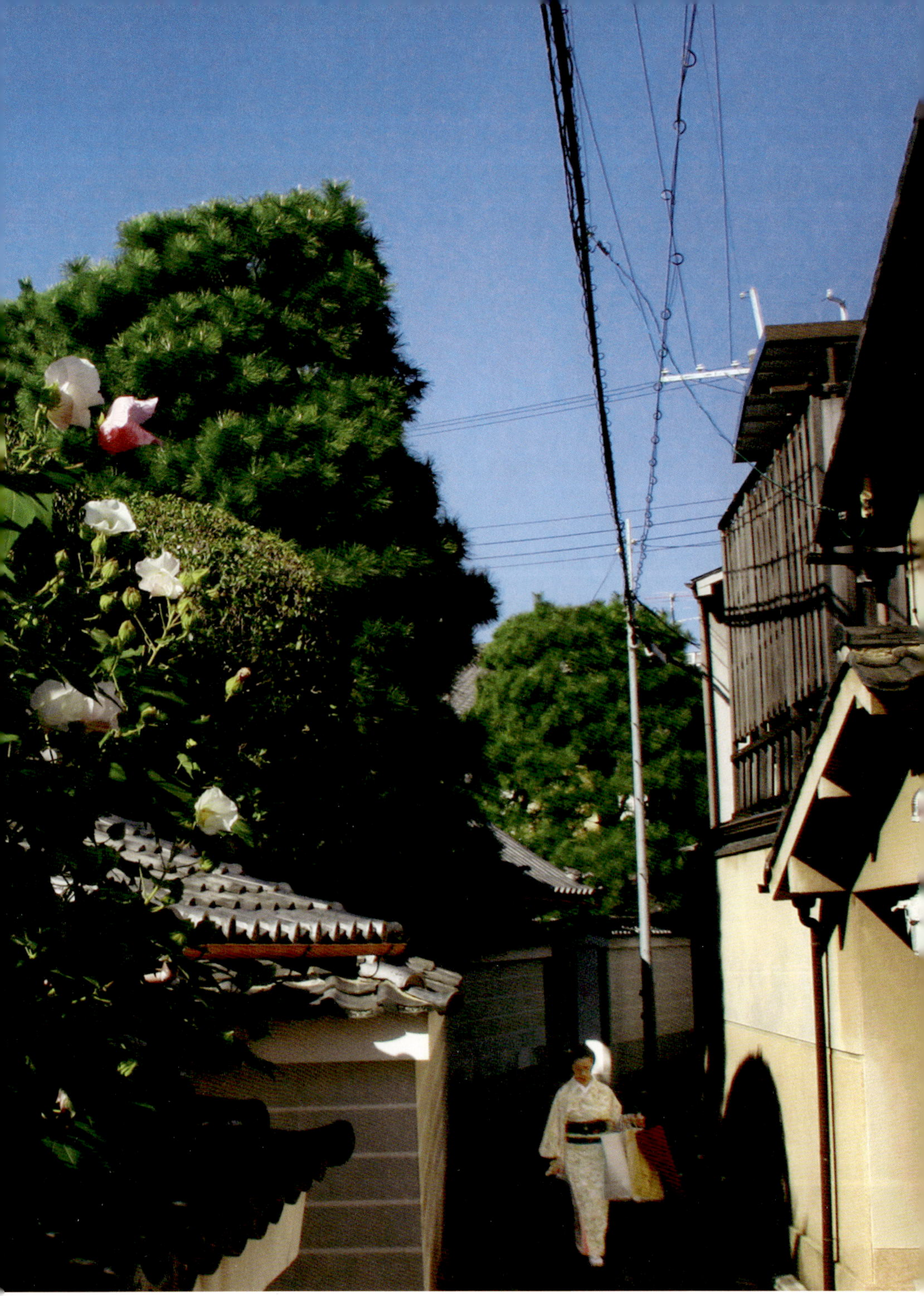

ビアガーデン | Beer Garden

7月1日〜9月5日（上七軒）／7月中旬〜8月中旬（宮川町）
芸妓、舞妓がもてなす花街のビアガーデン。

July 1- Sept. 5 (Kamishichiken)
Mid-July - Mid-August (Miyagawacho)

Special summer beer garden in Kagai. Geiko and maiko come to every table and diners can enjoy conversing with them.

上七軒のビアガーデン | Beer garden in Kamishichiken　上七軒 | Kamishichiken

宮川町のビアガーデン ｜ Beer garden in Miyagawacho　宮川町 ｜ Miyagawacho

ゆかた会 | Yukata-kai

7月中旬(宮川町)／7月下旬(祇園東)

芸妓、舞妓の日頃のお稽古の成果を発表する勉強会。

Mid-July (Miyagawacho), Late July (Gion Higashi)

During this event, geiko and maiko display their skills on traditional Japanese musical instruments (with the Japanese whistle, small hand drum, drum, etc.) and dance while wearing yukata summer kimono.

揃いのゆかたで | Everyone is dressed in the same yukata summer kimono　祇園東 | Gion Higashi

ゆかた会の日 | The day of Yukata-kai　祇園東 | Gion Higashi

瑞饋祭 | Zuiki Festival

10月1日～5日(上七軒)

北野天満宮の秋の大祭。平安後期から記録にある古い祭礼で、五穀豊穣に感謝して行われる。4日、御旅所から北野天満宮へ向かう瑞饋御輿や三基の御鳳輦の行列が上七軒の街を通り、氏子である芸妓、舞妓たちはお茶屋の玄関先に出てきて行列を出迎える。

October 1-5(Kamishichiken)

This is an old autumn harvest festival at Kitano Tenmangu Shrine originating in the late Heian period (794-1185). People show their gratitude for a good autumn harvest to the deity. On the 4th, a mikoshi portable shrine decorated with vegetables and floats depart from the shrine hall called Otabisho to the main shrine passing through the Kamishichiken district. Geiko and maiko come out of ochaya and welcome the procession.

お茶屋には祭の暖簾や提灯がかかる | Ochaya hang special entrance curtains and lanterns for the festival
上七軒 | Kamishichiken

瑞饋御輿 | Mikoshi portable shrine in Zuiki Festival　上七軒 | Kamishichiken

祇園新橋の夕日と石畳 | Stone-paved street in Gion Shinbashi in the evening sun

時代祭 | Jidai Festival

10月22日（祇園甲部・宮川町・先斗町・上七軒・祇園東）

October 22 (Gion Kobu, Miyagawacho, Pontocho, Kamishichiken, Gion Higashi)

明治28年（1895）平安神宮が創建された際、始められた祭。京都御苑から平安神宮まで練り歩く時代行列で知られる。各花街は交替でこの行列に参加し、芸妓、舞妓たちが巴御前や清少納言、小野小町などに扮する。

The Jidai Festival started in 1895 to commemorate the establishment of Heian Shrine. The festival procession, featuring authentic costumes from all of Kyoto's historical periods, proceeds from the Kyoto Imperial Palace to Heian Shrine. Every year, geiko and maiko dress up in the costumes of famous historical figures.

「巴御前」に扮して | Maiko disguising as Tomoe Gozen (a female warrior in the Heian Period)

宮川町 | Miyagawacho

かにかくに祭 | Kanikakuni Festival

11月8日（祇園甲部）

祇園を愛した歌人吉井勇を偲んで、吉井勇が定宿とした「大友」跡にある歌碑に菊の花を献花する。歌碑には吉井勇の「かにかくに　祇園はこひし　寝るときも　枕のしたを　水のながるる」という歌が刻まれている。

November 8 (Gion Kobu)

In memory of the famous poet, Isamu Yoshii (1886-1960), and his great love for Gion, geiko and maiko offer chrysanthemum flowers to him at a stone monument located near the Tatsumi Bridge along the Shirakawa Stream. The name of the event, Kanikakuni, is taken from one of the lines engraved on the stone. Yoshii writes: "I miss Gion so much. I can hear the sound of Shirakawa Stream while I am in bed."

歌碑は白川沿いにある | Stone monument by Shirakawa Stream　　祇園甲部 | Gion Kobu

お茶の接待も行われる | Maiko and geiko performing tea ceremony　祇園甲部 | Gion Kobu

祇園をどりの頃の祇園会館｜Gion Kaikan Hall around the time of Gion Odori

祇園小唄祭 | Gion Kouta Festival

11月23日（祇園甲部・宮川町・先斗町・上七軒・祇園東）

円山公園の祇園しだれ桜のそばに祇園小唄の歌碑がある。「祇園小唄」は作家・長田幹彦が祇園のお茶屋「吉うた」に滞在しているとき作詞し、佐々紅華が作曲した昭和の名曲。この名曲の功績を改めて顕彰しようと、舞妓による献花と、歌詞の朗読がある。

November 23 (Gion Kobu, Miyagawacho, Pontocho, Kamishichiken, Gion Higashi)

There is a stone monument dedicated to the Gion Kouta (the best known Kagai song; lyrics by Mikihiko Nagata and music by Koka Sassa) in Maruyama Park. This festival started in order to show the important contribution this song has made to the Kagai. During the festival, maiko offer flowers to the monument and read lyrics of the song out loud.

献花 | Dedicating flowers　　祇園東 | Gion Higashi

北野献茶祭 | Kitano Tea Dedication Festival

12月1日(上七軒)

天正15年(1587)に豊臣秀吉が催した「北野大茶湯」にちなみ北野天満宮本殿にて行われる大茶会。当日は上七軒歌舞練場にも副席が設けられ、色紋付の芸妓、舞妓が立礼でお茶を点て、接客する。

December 1 (Kamishichiken)

Hideyoshi Toyotomi, one of Japan's most powerful warlords, held a huge public tea ceremony party at Kitano Tenmangu Shrine in 1587. This tea ceremony festival recreates the feeling of the original party and is held at the main shrine hall. Additional seats are set up in the Kamishichiken Kaburenjo Theatre where geiko and maiko in formal kimono offer matcha green tea in the Ryurei style (table style) to the public.

上七軒歌舞練場での副席 | Tea ceremony performed in the Kamishichiken Kaburenjo Theatre
上七軒 | Kamishichiken

顔見世総見 | Kaomise Soken

12月初旬（祇園甲部・宮川町・先斗町・上七軒・祇園東）

Early December (Gion Kobu, Miyagawacho, Pontocho, Kamishichiken, Gion Higashi)

11月末、南座に「まねき（役者の名を書いた看板）」があがる。毎年11月30日から27日間にわたって行われる顔見世は東西の人気役者が顔を揃える歌舞伎興行で、京都の師走の風物詩となっている。興行中の5日間、各花街ごとに芸妓、舞妓たちが揃って観劇し、これを顔見世総見という。

At the end of November, the famous Minamiza Theatre hangs out the annual kabuki maneki, wooden signboards that announce the names of the performers in the Kaomise performance. Starting from November 30th, the best kabuki actors come to Kyoto for 27 days to perform. For 5 days during the performance period, geiko and maiko from each Kagai come and watch the stage (Kaomise Soken).

総見に向かう朝 | Going to the Kaomise Soken kabuki watching　先斗町 | Pontocho

まねきのあがる南座 | Minamiza Theatre with Maneki (wooden signboards with the names of the performers in the Kaomise performance)
祇園甲部 | Gion Kobu

「まねき」のかんざしには好きな役者にサインをいれてもらう
Maiko goes to her favorite kabuki actor and gets his autograph on the hair ornament

宮川町 | Miyagawacho

初雪の上七軒 | First snow of the year in Kamishichiken

上七軒おもちつき | Kamishichiken Rice Pounding Event

12月中旬（上七軒）

地域の人々との交流の場ともなり、なごやかな雰囲気につつまれる。

Mid-December (Kamishichiken)

Geiko and maiko in Kamishichiken enjoy rice pounding and making rice cakes together with local people.

お餅をつく舞妓の姿も | Maiko pounding rice cake　　上七軒 | Kamishichiken

事始め | Kotohajime

12月13日（祇園甲部・宮川町・先斗町・上七軒・祇園東）

この日から正月の準備（事）を始めるので、事始めという。日頃お世話になっているお師匠さんやお茶屋などに、裏白とゆずり葉を敷いた鏡餅をおさめ、ご挨拶をする。お師匠さんは舞扇を手渡して一年の労をねぎらう。

December 13 (Gion Kobu, Miyagawacho, Pontocho, Kamishichiken, Gion Higashi)

Kotohajime literally translated means "things to do for the New Year." As a part of the New Year preparations, geiko and maiko show their best wishes by offering specially decorated gifts of New Year's rice cakes for good relations in the coming year to their teachers and ochaya they feel indebted to. The teacher hands them a folding fan one by one and reward their effort for the past year.

舞扇を手渡す京舞井上流五世家元井上八千代
The master of Inoue School of Dance hands a folding fan to every geiko and maiko
祇園甲部 | Gion Kobu

挨拶がとびかう | Year-end Greetings　先斗町 | Pontocho

先斗町の提灯 | A lantern of Pontocho

おことうさん | Okotosan

12月31日（祇園甲部・宮川町）

日頃お世話になっているお茶屋に「お事多うさんどす」と年末の挨拶廻りをする。お茶屋では「福玉」を用意して、挨拶に来た妓に渡す。中には身の回りの小物などが入っている。

December 31 (Gion Kobu, Miyagawacho)

Okotosan is the year-end greeting when each geiko and maiko visits ochaya with the greeting "Okotosan-dosu." Here she receives a fukudama (ball shaped bag) containing small daily items.

福玉を持って | Going out with fuku-dama　祇園甲部 | Gion Kobu

をけら詣り | Okera Mairi

12月31日（祇園甲部・宮川町）

December 31 (Gion Kobu, Miyagawacho)

31日の夜、八坂神社は無病息災の御利益があるという「をけら火」をもらう「をけら詣り」の人々で賑わう。近年は里帰りする舞妓も多くなり、「をけら詣り」をする舞妓の姿を見ることは少なくなった。

On the night of December 31, a number of people visit Yasaka Shrine and light a straw rope from the shrine lantern. The fire is called Okera-bi and is believed to provide a healthy life during the coming year. Some maiko visit Yasaka Shrine for Okera-bi, but in recent years the number became less as many of maiko return to their hometown during the New Year's period.

吉兆縄に「をけら火」を移し、持って帰る | Get the rope lit with Okera-bi and bring it back home
宮川町 | Miyagawacho

176

稽古（四世 井上八千代師）
The 4th Yachiyo Inoue, the master of Inoue School of Dance

第四章 昭和四〜昭和六 祇園

Chapter 4

雨の花見小路 | Hanamikoji Street in rain

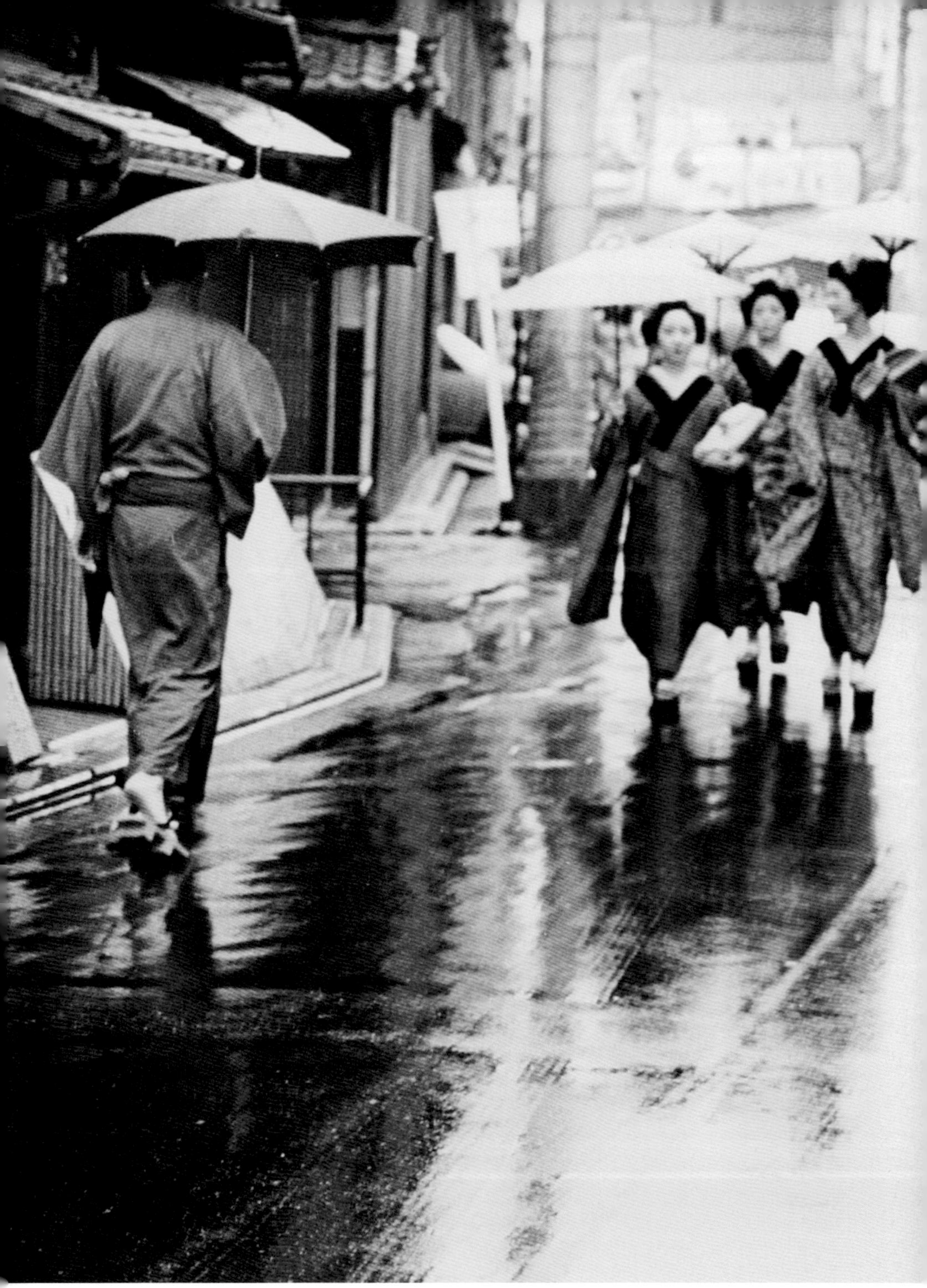

夕刊持って | Chatting on the street with a newspaper in the hand

玄関にて | Getting ready at the entrance

夕方の花見小路 | Hanamikoji Street in the evening

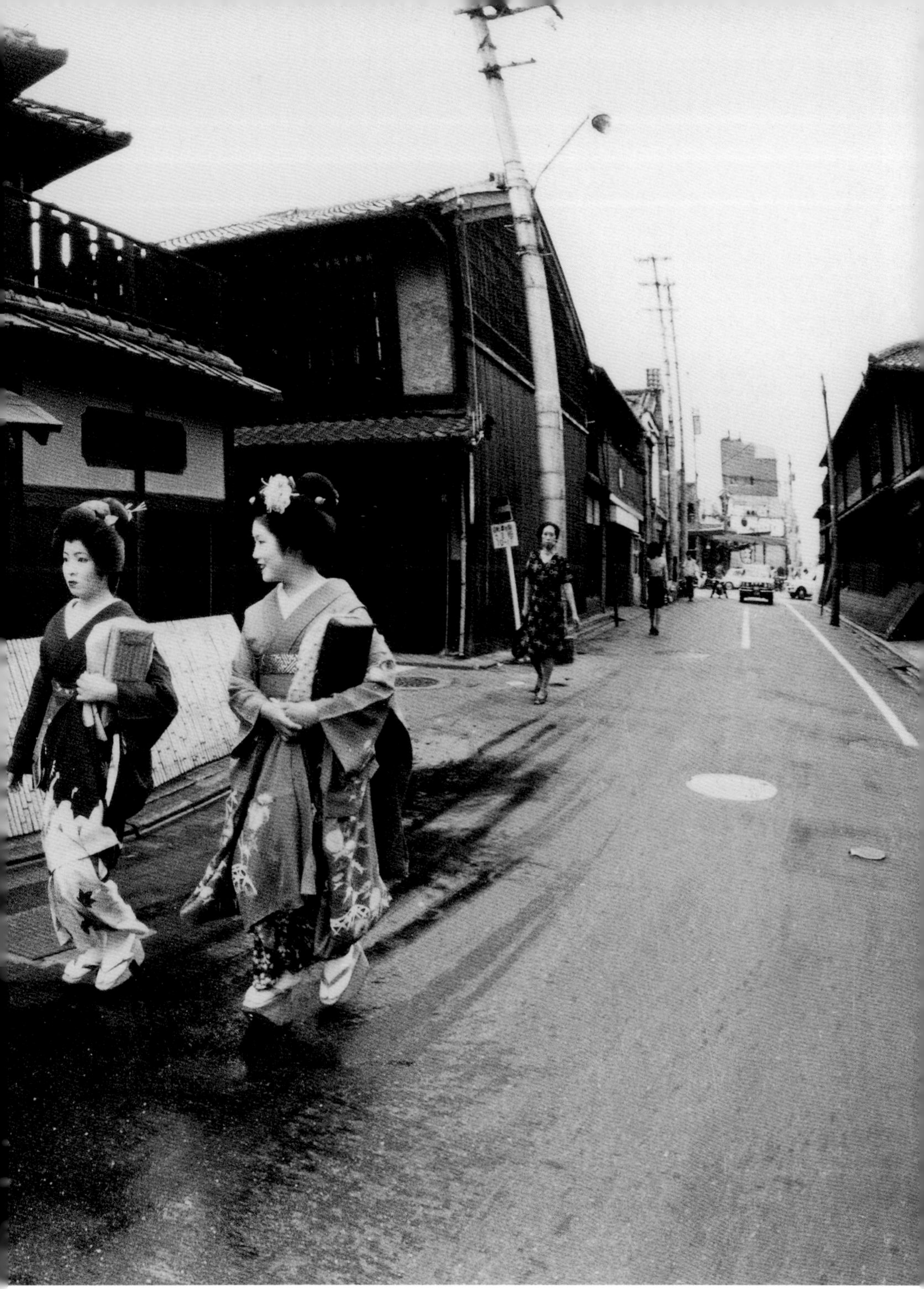

傘 | With umbrella

かにかくに祭にて | Tea ceremony performed in Kanikakuni Festival

事始めの朝 | Morning of Kotohajime

稲穂のかんざし | Hair ornament with real rice stalk

路地を行く | Going a backstreet

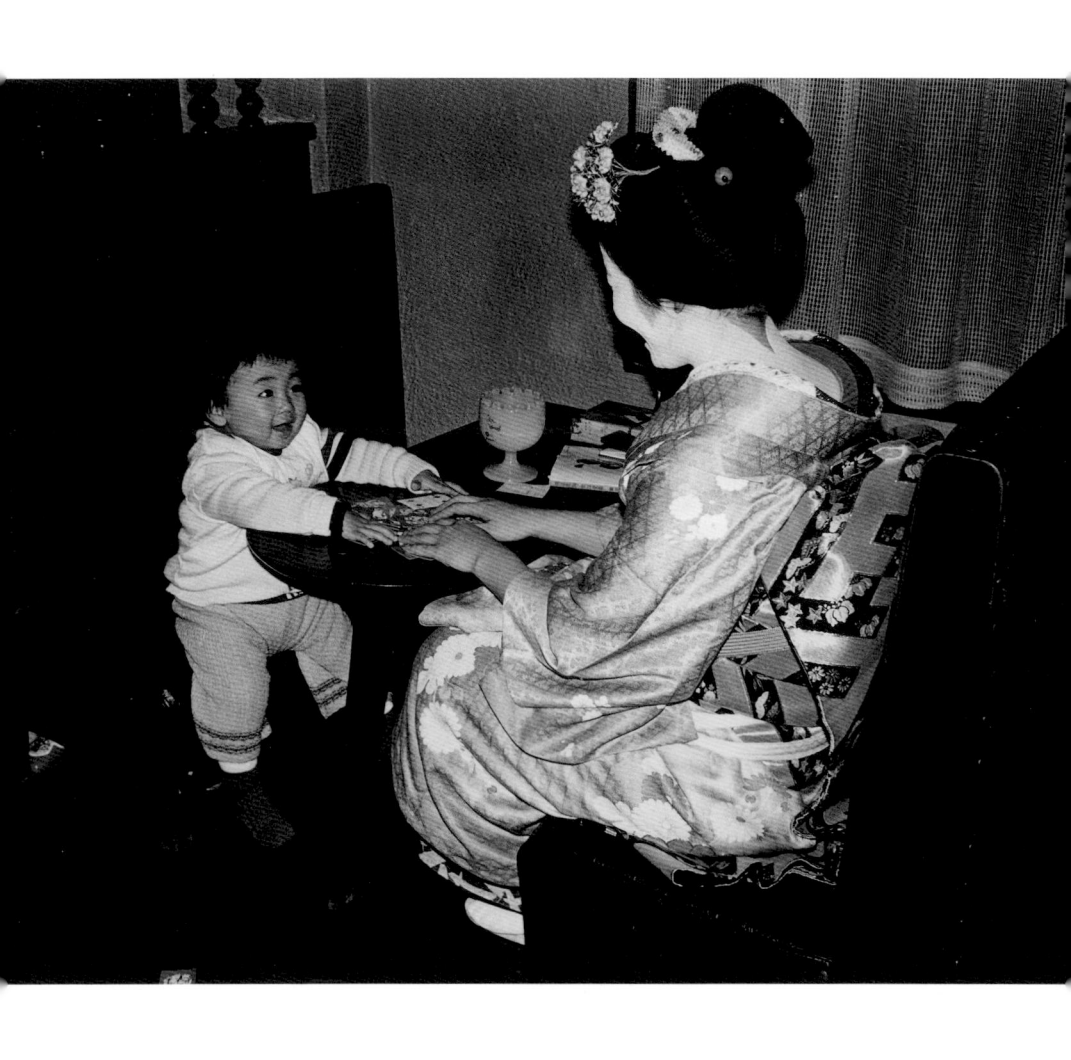

喫茶たんぽぽにて | At Café Tampopo

節分「お化け」 | Obake disguise at Setsubun

急ぎお茶屋へ | Hurrying to work

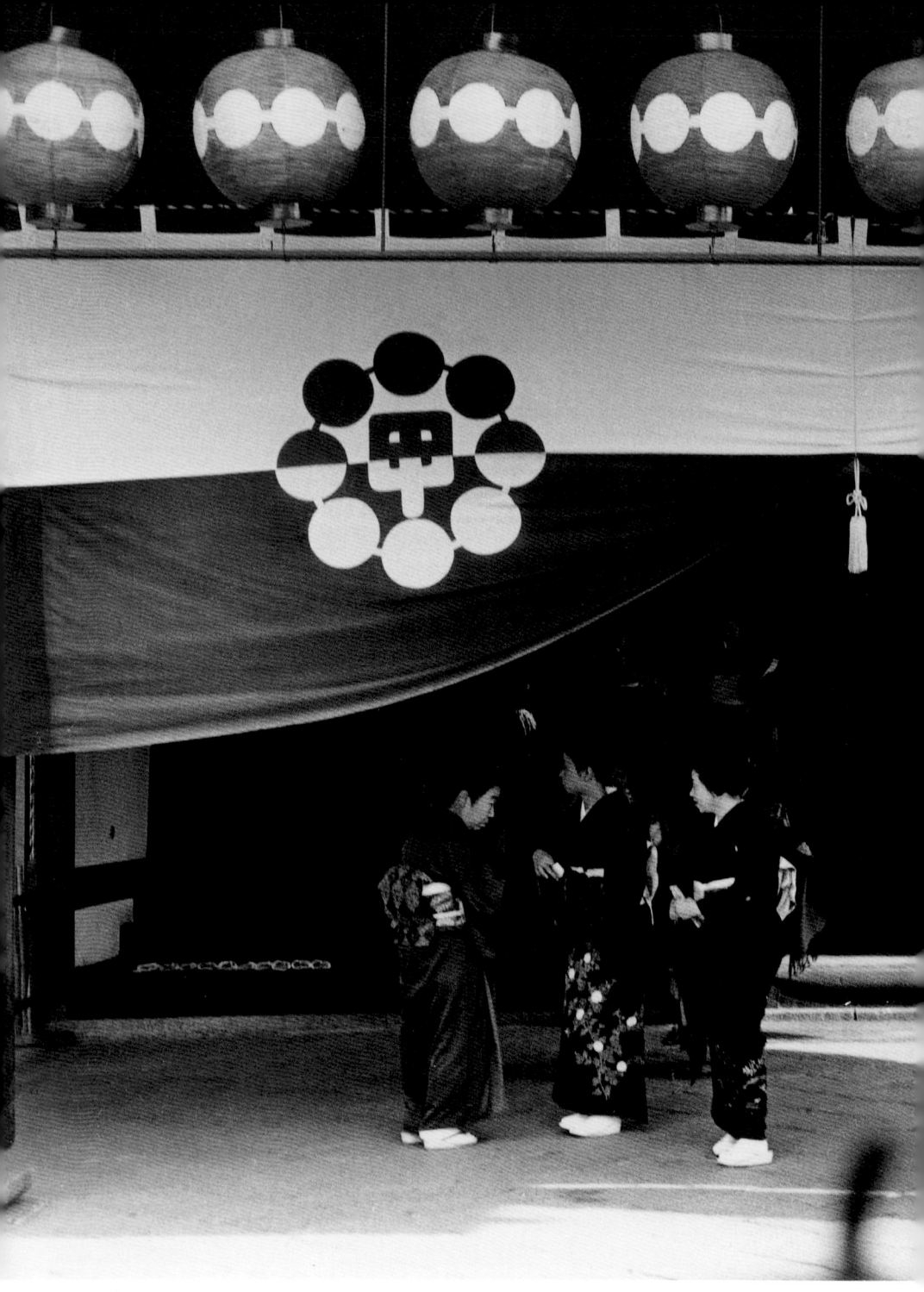

始業式 | Shigyoshiki Year Opening Ceremony

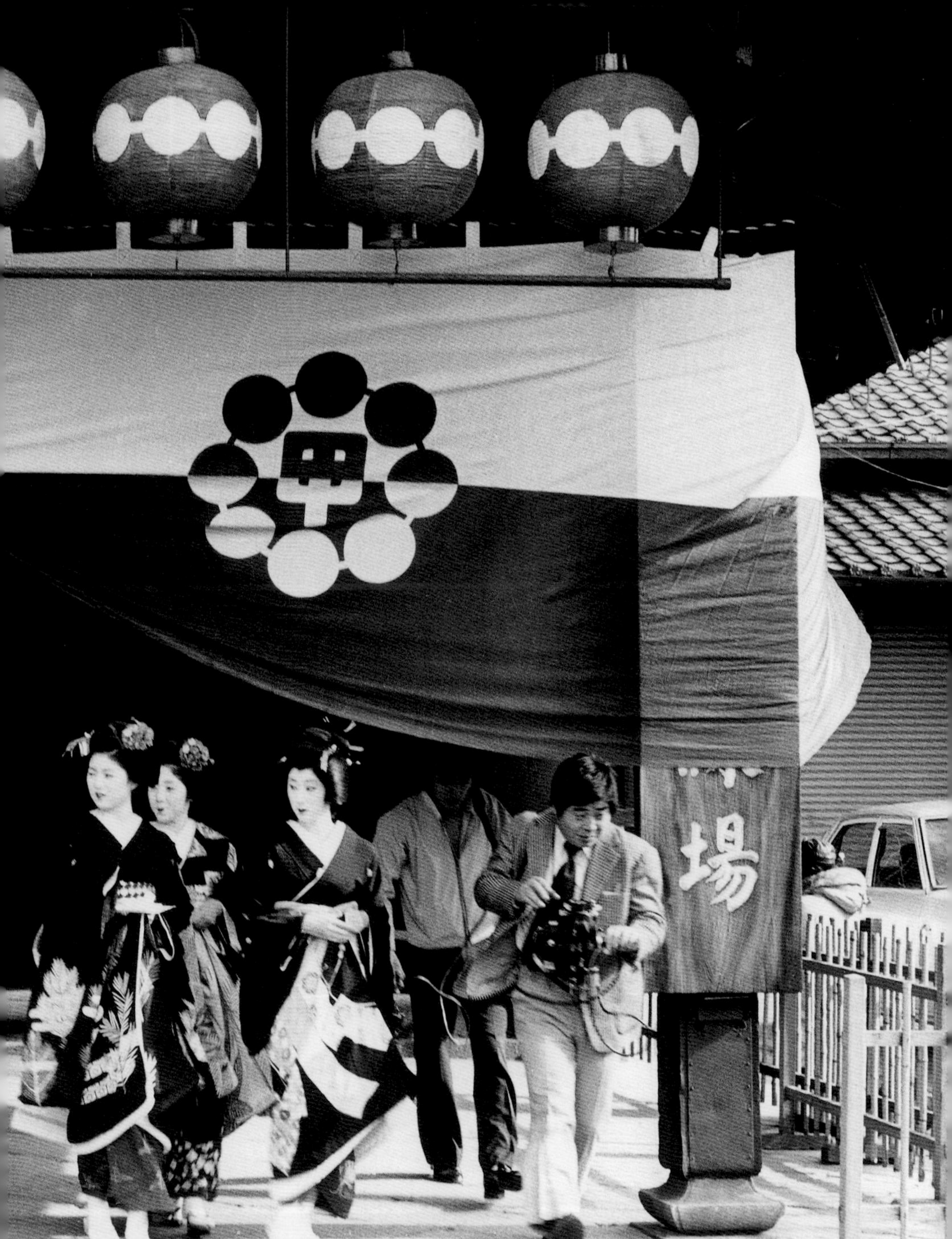
甲
場

八朔 | Hassaku Summer Greetings

八朔の日　喫茶たんぽぽにて | On the day of Hassaku, at Café Tampopo

年始廻り お茶屋玄関にて | New Year's greeting at the entrance of ochaya

女紅場入口 | Entrance of Nyokoba (center for women's education)

大雨の女紅場入口 | Entrance of Nyokoba in the heavy rain

都をどりへ | Heading to Miyako Odori

温習会 楽屋 | Dressing room (Onshu-kai)

温習会 楽屋 | Dressing room (Onshu-kai)

温習会 楽屋 | Dressing room (Onshu-kai)

雪の祇園白川畔 | Gion Shirakawa in snow

半だら | Han-dara (just before becoming a maiko)

お茶屋にて | At ochaya

お茶屋にて | At ochaya

温習会 本番前 | Last minute before the Onshu-kai stage

店出しの日 | Day of Misedashi

店出しの日 | Day of Misedashi

都をどり稽古 | Practice for Miyako Odori

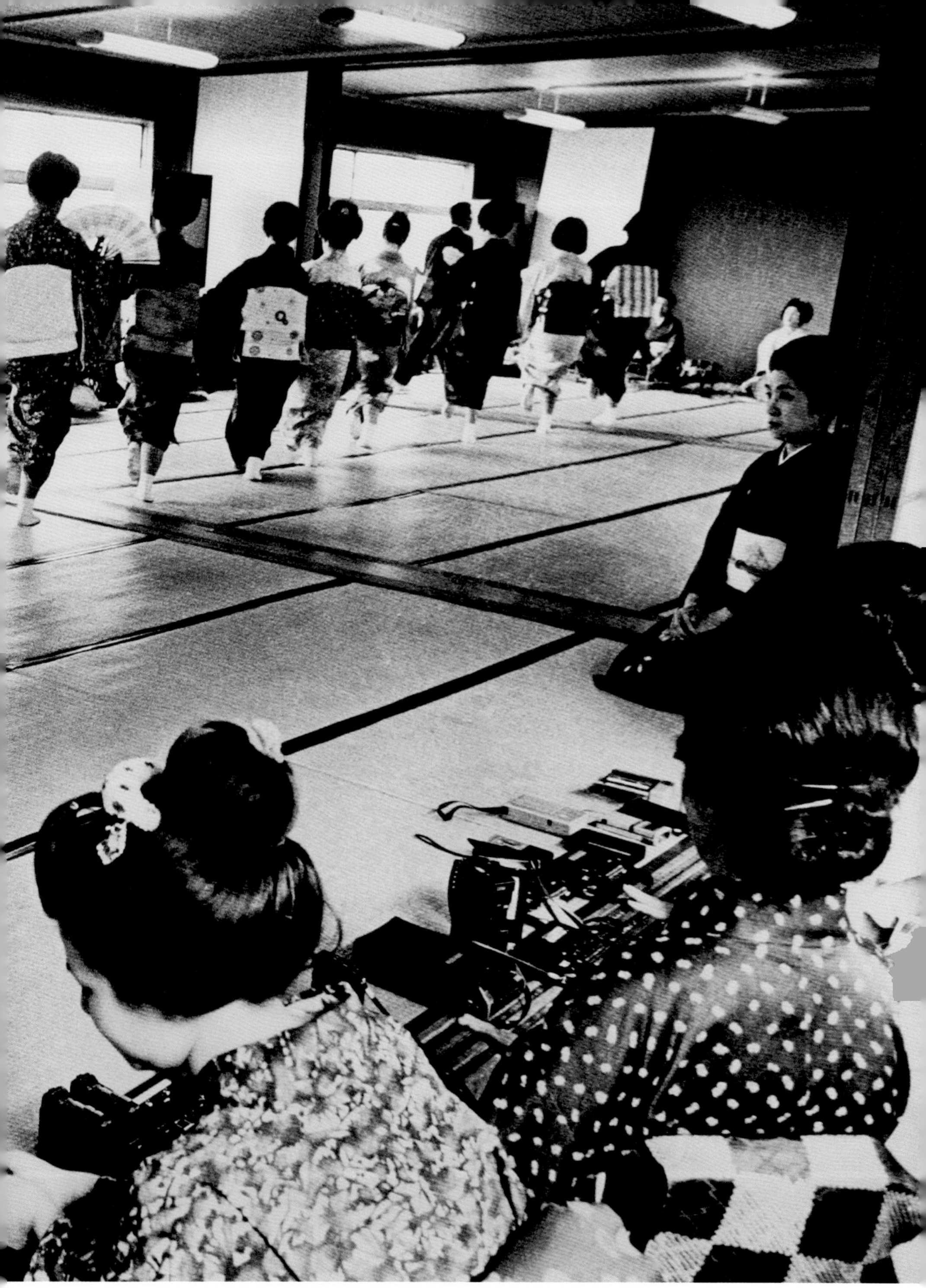

都をどり | Miyako Odori

晴れの日 | A fine day

雨の日の八朔 | Hassaku on rainy day

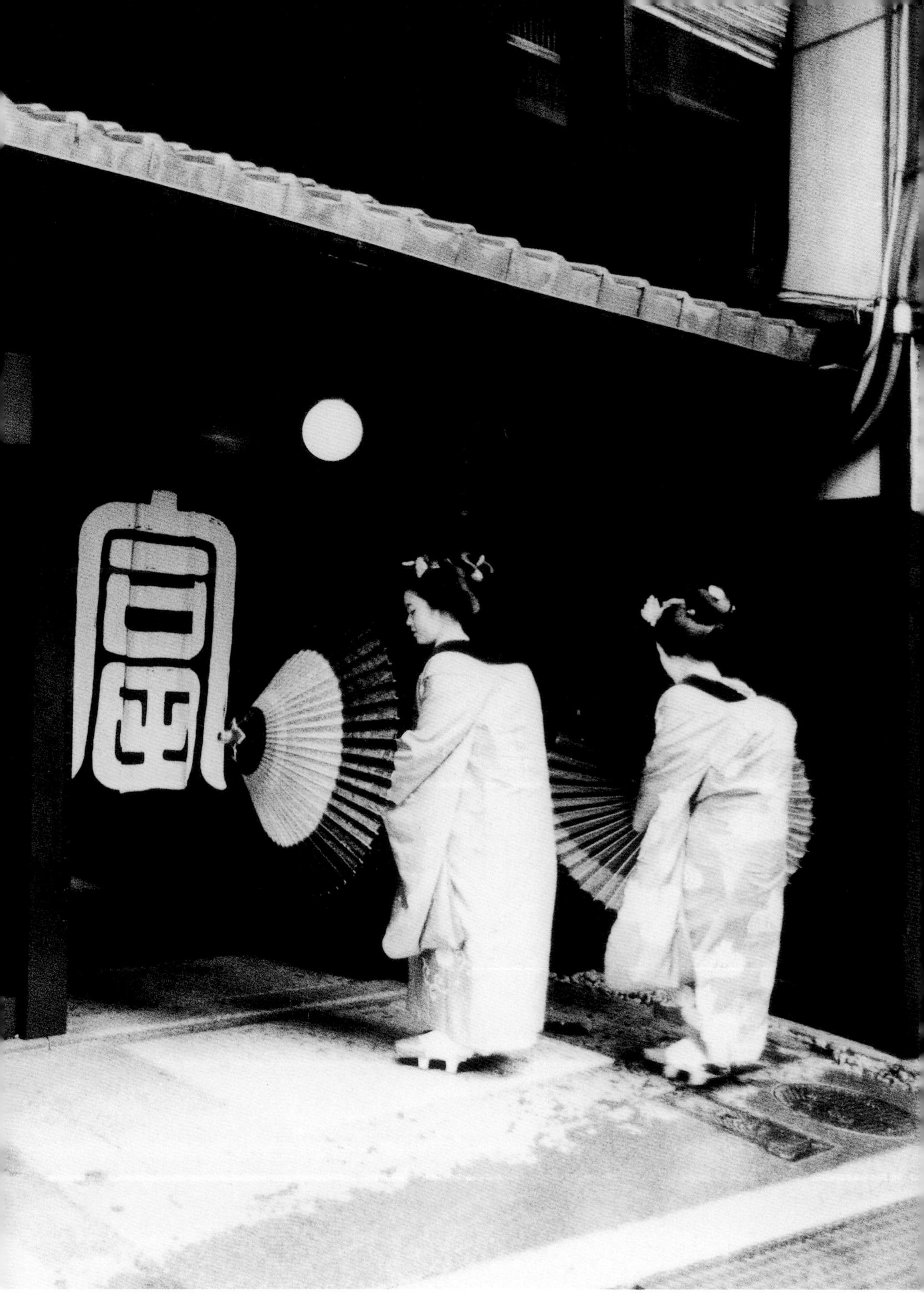

立ち話 | Chat on the street

顔見世総見 | Kaomise Soken

春の祇園白川 | Gion Shirakawa in spring

お礼まいり │ Orei Mairi (pay a visit of thanks to the master of dance after Miyako Odori)

髪結い | Kamiyui fixing hair

お座敷 | In the ozashiki

稽古（四世 井上八千代師） | The 4th Yachiyo Inoue, the master of Inoue School of Dance, giving training

稽古 | Dance practice

写真リスト

頁	キャプション	撮影年月
177	稽古(四世 井上八千代師)	1985(昭和60)年1月
178-179	雨の花見小路	1973(昭和48)年6月
180	夕刊持って	1973(昭和48)年6月
181	玄関にて	1973(昭和48)年6月
182-183	夕方の花見小路	1973(昭和48)年7月
184	傘	1973(昭和48)年9月
185	かにかくに祭にて	1973(昭和48)年11月
186	事始めの朝	1973(昭和48)年12月
187	稲穂のかんざし	1974(昭和49)年1月
188	路地を行く	1974(昭和49)年3月
189	喫茶たんぽぽにて	1975(昭和50)年2月
190	節分「お化け」	1975(昭和50)年2月
191	急ぎお茶屋へ	1975(昭和50)年6月
192-193	始業式	1976(昭和51)年1月
194	八朔	1976(昭和51)年8月
195	八朔の日 喫茶たんぽぽにて	1976(昭和51)年8月
196	年始廻り お茶屋玄関にて	1977(昭和52)年1月
197	女紅場入口	1977(昭和52)年4月
198	大雨の女紅場入口	1977(昭和52)年4月
199	都をどりへ	1977(昭和52)年4月
200	温習会 楽屋	1976(昭和51)年10月
201	温習会 楽屋	1977(昭和52)年10月
202	温習会 楽屋	1977(昭和52)年10月
203	雪の祇園白川畔	1978(昭和53)年頃
204	半だら	1978(昭和53)年3月
205	お茶屋にて	1978(昭和53)年7月
206	お茶屋にて	1978(昭和53)年8月
207	温習会 本番前	1981(昭和56)年10月
208	店出しの日	1980(昭和55)年3月
209	店出しの日	1980(昭和55)年3月
210-211	都をどり稽古	1982(昭和57)年3月
212	都をどり	1982(昭和57)年4月
213	晴れの日	1983(昭和58)年秋
214-215	雨の日の八朔	1982(昭和57)年8月
216	立ち話	1983(昭和58)年10月
217	顔見世総見	1983(昭和58)年12月
218	春の祇園白川	1984(昭和59)年4月
219	お礼まいり	1984(昭和59)年5月
220	髪結い	1984(昭和59)年10月
221	お座敷	1985(昭和60)年9月
222	稽古(四世 井上八千代師)	1985(昭和60)年1月
223	稽古	1985(昭和60)年1月

※写真は全て祇園甲部です。

第五章 Chapter 5

Transition from Maiko to Geiko
– The 5 year record of Satsuki in Gion Kobu

舞妓から芸妓へ
―祇園甲部・紗月の5年間―

※第五章は『美しいキモノ』(ハースト婦人画報社)の連載企画を再構成したものです。

仕込みさんの頃
Satsuki in the Shikomi period (training for becoming a maiko)

2010年3月

紗月(さつき) | Satsuki

中学2年生の夏頃から祇園甲部の屋方（置屋）「つる居」さんに通い、舞のお稽古をスタート。中学卒業後、「つる居」にて、仕込みさんとして住み込みで修業を始め、見習いさんを経て、2011年2月28日に「店出し」をして舞妓に。2015年2月23日に「衿替え」をして芸妓になった。前ページの写真は「衿替え」の時に着た着物。紗月の名にちなみ「月」が描かれている。

Since she was around 13 years old, Satsuki started her Japanese dance lesson at Tsurui, one of the okiya in Gion Kobu, with a wish to be a maiko. After she finished compulsory education at the age of 15, she moved to Tsurui and started her full time training. After one year as a Shikomi (trainee before maiko), she made her debut as maiko on February 28th, 2011. She had her celebratory Erikae (transition from maiko to geiko) on February 23rd, 2015, and her career as a geiko has begun. The kimono on previous page is the one Satsuki wore for her Erikae. As her name contains a Chinese character representing "moon," the kimono has a beautiful moon design.

仕込みさんの頃。八朔 | In the Shikomi period (on the day of Hassaku Summer Greeting)　2010年8月

仕込みさんの頃。井上八千代師宅に新年のご挨拶に行く「初寄り」の日。
華やかなお引きずりの着物をきたお姉さんたちと
In the Shikomi period; On the day of Hatsuyori New Year's Gathering

2011年1月

2011年1月

見習いさんの頃は、だらりの帯より短い半だらの帯
Satsuki wore "Han-dara" or half-length obi sash while she was in the Minarai period (just before the debut as a maiko)

店出し

仕込みさんと見習いさんの期間を経て、晴れて舞妓になることを「店出し」という。舞妓の名はお姉さん芸妓の名から一字もらうのが通例となっており、紗月さんの「紗」の字はお姉さんの紗矢佳さんからもらった。2011年2月28日、紗矢佳さんが芸妓となる「衿替え」と紗月さんの「店出し」が同時に行われた。ひとつの屋方から同じ日に「衿替え」と「店出し」が行われるのは、祇園甲部では38年ぶりであった。

髪結い

店出しの3日間は正装用の「割れしのぶ」。
早朝、髪結いさんに行って結ってもらう。

1
2 
3 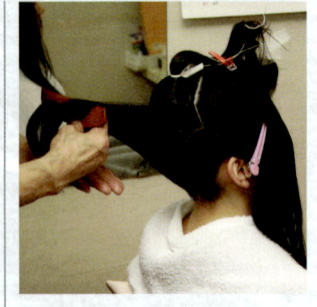
4 
5 
6 
7 
8 
9 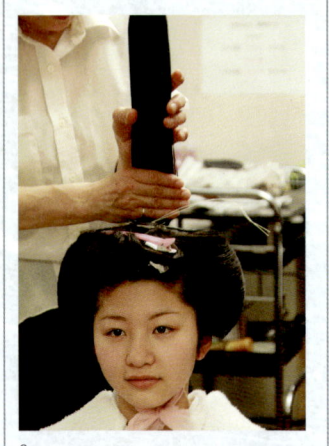

230

Misedashi – Official Debut as a Maiko

After a period as trainee, a maiko finally makes her debut which is called Misedashi. February 28th, 2011 was the big day for the okiya: Satsuki's Misedashi and another older maiko, Sayaka, had her Erikae (transition from maiko to geiko) on the same day. It was the first time in the past 38 years that an okiya in Gion Kobu had both Misedashi and Erikae on the same day.

Kamiyui Fixing Hair

For the first three days from Misedashi, a maiko has a hairstyle called Ware Shinobu in the special formal style. She goes to the hairdresser very early in the morning.

10

11

12

13

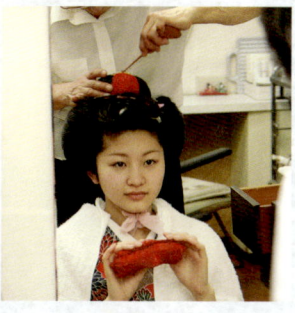

14

15

16

17

18

化粧

Makeup

「店出し」の日は顔師さんに化粧をしてもらうが、それ以降は自分ですることになる。ほんのりピンクを混ぜたおしろいを刷毛で塗り、眉や目じりにも紅をさしていく。襟足は通常2本だが、店出しなど特別な日は3本足に塗る。口紅は舞妓になってから1年間は下唇のみ（花街によっては違うところもある）。

A maiko has a special makeup staff to complete her face only on the day of Misedashi and she will do it by herself on every day after. They wear red rouge only on the bottom lip for the first year after Misedashi.

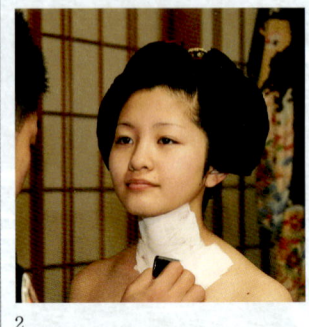

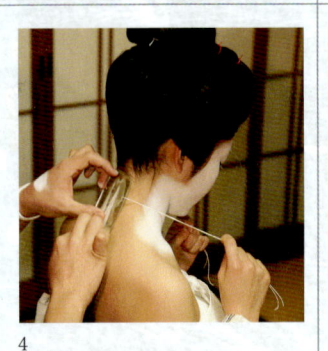

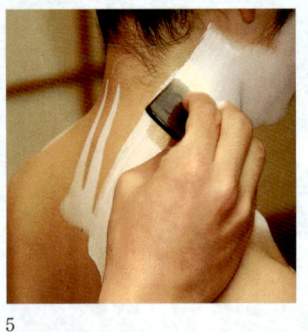

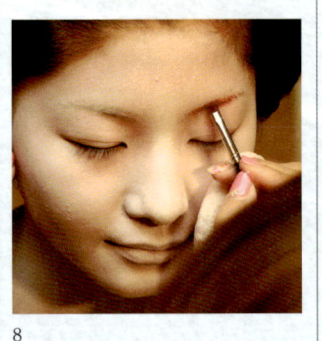

1

2

3

4

5

6

7

8

9

232

10

着付け
Kimono Dressing

男衆さんによって15分ほどで着付けてもらう。だらりの帯は締めるのに相当な力がいるという。黒紋付きの場合、舞妓はぽっちり（帯留）も帯締めもつけない。

The male specialist of taking care of maiko, called Otokoshi, quickly dress a maiko in about 15 minutes.

1

2

3

4

5

6

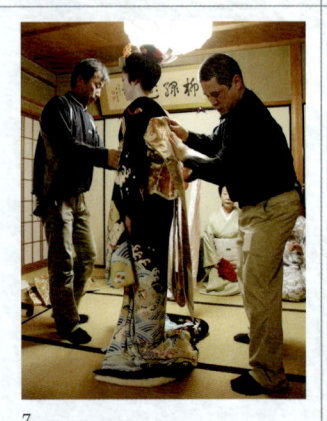

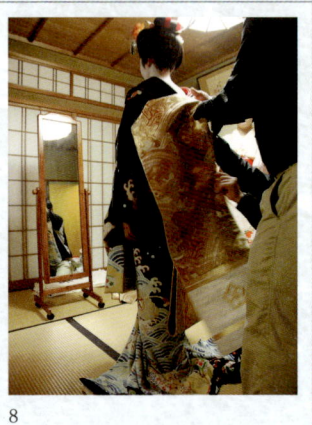

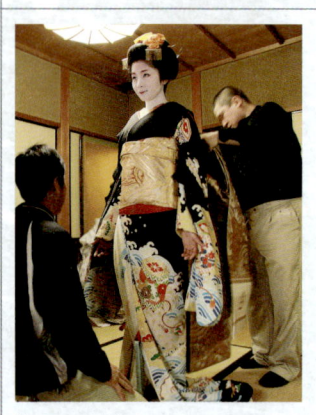

7

8

9

234

お姉さん芸妓の紗矢佳さんと | Satsuki with her elder geiko, Sayaka　2011年2月28日

びら（銀の挿しもの）を両方に挿すのは店出しの時だけ

Silver hair ornaments are set on both sides of hair only on the day of Misedashi

2011年2月28日

屋方のおかあさん | Satsuki's oka-san at her yakata　2011年2月28日

目録

Mokuroku

屋方の玄関に貼られているのは「目録」。店出しや衿替えを祝って、贔屓筋や、同じ花街のお姉さんなどから送られる。

The decorative poster-like item on the wall of the entrance is called Mokuroku. Their regular customers and older geiko in the same Kagai send celebratory Mokuroku to commemorate the event of Misedashi and Erikae.

挨拶まわりへ | Setting off to courtesy visits in the neighborhood　2011年2月28日

祇園町を行く | Walking in Gion district　2011年2月28日

紗矢佳さんと固めの盃を交わす │ Satsuki exchanging cups of sake with Sayaka, her elder geiko, as a pledge of partnership

240

2011年2月28日

翌日のお礼参り | The day after Misedashi, Satsuki visited neighborhood and showed her gratitude for the Misedashi ceremony
2011年3月1日

お礼にうかがう時は半だらの帯で | Wear Han-dara (half-length sash) on the day of paying courtesy visits of thanks

2011年3月1日

"姉妹"で都をどりの楽屋入り | Satsuki and Sayaka going to perform in the Miyako Odori Performance
2011年4月

都をどり お茶席の日 | On the day Satsuki served tea for visitors during the Miyako Odori Performance

2011年4月

歌舞練場の庭園にて | In the garden of Gion Kobu Kaburenjo Theatre　2011年4月

夏のひとこま | A summer day　2011年6月

みやび会 | Miyabi-kai　2011年7月

夏のお座敷 | Entertaining people in an ozashiki in summer　2011年7月

祇園祭 宵々山 | Yoi-yoi-yama (festival eve) of Gion Festival　2011年7月

祇園祭 巡行 | Grand procession of Gion Festival　2011年7月

八朔 | Hassaku Summer Greetings　2011年8月

八朔 | Hassaku Summer Greetings　2011年8月

時代祭 | Jidai Festival　2011年10月

顔見世総見 | Kaomise Soken Kabuki Watching　2011年12月

事始め | Kotohajime　2011年12月

福玉を持って | Walking with fuku-dama in her hand　2011年12月

初寄り ｜ Hatsuyori New Year Gathering　2012年1月

「お化け」で「お染久松」の「お染」に扮して | Obake Disguise　2012年2月

2年目に入り、上唇にも紅をさすようになった
From second year, Satsuki started to wear rouge on her upper lip

2012年3月

2012年3月

都をどり舞台稽古。初舞台にむけて練習を積む
Practice for Miyako Odori Performance; Hard practice continues every day

紗矢佳さんと料亭「祇園丸山」にて
With Sayaka, at a high-class Japanese restaurant, Gion Maruyama

2012年7月

喫茶店「切通し進々堂」の前で | In front of Café Kiridoshi Shinshindo　2012年7月

同じ屋方の杏佳さん姉さん、衿替えの日 | Elder maiko, Kyoka, had her day of Erikae (transition from maiko to geiko)
2012年10月

始業式にて表彰される | Receiving the award in Shigyoshiki Year Opening Ceremony
2013年1月

初寄り | Hatsuyori New Year Gathering　2013年1月

2013年4月

舞妓3年目。都をどりの舞台
Third year as a maiko; On the stage of Miyako Odori Performance

初めて「勝山」に結う。「勝山」は年長の舞妓が祇園祭の頃にのみ結う髪型

Satsuki's first hair set with the hairstyle of Katsuyama; Katsuyama is the style older maiko wear only during the Gion Festival

2013年7月

事始め│Kotohajime Year-end Preparation　2013年12月

紗月さん舞妓4年目。同じ屋方の茉利佳ちゃん、店出しの日　　2014年5月
Fourth year as a maiko; A younger maiko, Marika, celebrated her Misedashi (debut as a maiko)

祇園祭　花傘巡行 | Hanagasa Junko Procession in Gion Festival　2014年7月

料亭旅館「祇園畑中」にて | At a high-class Japanese restaurant, Gion Hatanaka　2014年8月

温習会の舞台に立つ | Performing in the Onshu-kai stage　2014年10月

始業式 | Shigyoshiki Year Opening Ceremony　2015年1月

始業式 | Shigyoshiki Year Opening Ceremony　2015年1月

先笄

2015年2月15日、衿替えを間近に控え、舞妓最後の髪型、先笄を結うことになった。先笄を結いお歯黒をした紗月さんは、ぐっと大人っぽい雰囲気に。

Sakko

On February 15th, 2015, Satuki had a special hairstyle called Sakko for the last time as a maiko. With the Sakko hairstyle and teeth painted black (a traditional sign of a mature woman), Satsuki truly looked mature.

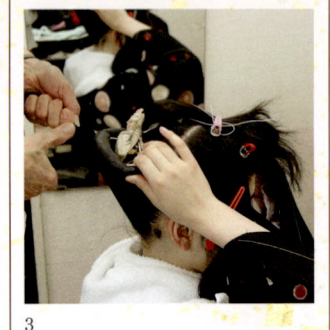

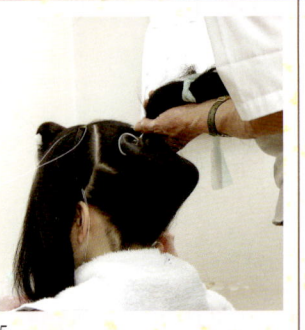

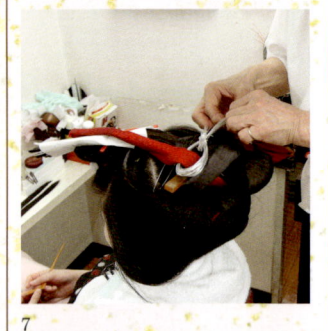

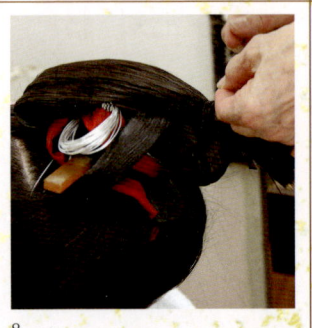

1

2

3

4

5

6

7

8

9

お歯黒

Ohaguro (painted teeth in black as a sign of matured woman)

276

「黒髪」を舞う | Performing a dance titled "Kuro-kami (Black Hair)"

衿替え

芸妓としてのお披露目を「衿替え」という。芸妓になる時期は屋方など関係者が相談して決めるが、舞妓になって4～5年目が多い。2015年2月23日、紗月さんは衿替えの日を迎えた。

化粧
Makeup

顔師さんに化粧をしてもらうが、口紅は自分でさす。舞妓は地毛で髪を結うが、芸妓はかつらとなる。

Maiko makes hairstyle with her own hair while geiko wears a wig.

1

2

3

4

5

6

7

8

278

Erikae – Transition from a Maiko to Geiko

Transition from maiko to geiko is called Erikae. Important people around the maiko including the okiya manager discuss and decide the timing, but in general, a maiko spends 3 to 4 years before Erikae. On February 23rd, 2015, Satsuki celebrated her Erikae.

着付け

Kimono Dressing

男衆さんに着付けてもらう。この日のために屋方のおかあさんが新調してくれた黒紋付きに身をつつむ。

Satsuki dressed in an elaborate formal black kimono newly made for her by her oka-san (female manager of yakata).

1

2

3

4

5

6

7

8

9

金屏風の前で │ In front of the gold folding screen　2015年2月23日

井上流では、芸妓になると、舞扇が舞妓のときの金地近衛引紅段紋入から、金地近衛引紫段紋入に変わる

According to the tradition of Inoue School of dance, a maiko uses a folding fan with red lines while a geiko uses the one with purple lines.

2015年2月23日

屋方のおかあさん、お姉さんにご挨拶 | Satsuki showing her gratitude to her oka-san and elder geiko
2015年2月23日

挨拶廻りに | Setting off for courtesy visits in the neighborhood　2015年2月23日

紗月さんの衿替えを一目見ようと、沿道には多くの人がつめかけた

A number of people gathered and waited to see Satsuki's Erikae　　　　　　2015年2月23日

男衆さんと挨拶に廻る | Going around the neighborhood with Otokoshi　2015年2月23日

2015年2月24日

翌日のお礼参り。夜はまた黒紋付の正装となる
The day after Erikae, Satsuki visited her neighborhood and showed her gratitude for the Erikae ceremony.
She got changed to the most formal black kimono in the evening.

色紋付 | Colored kimono with crest　2015年2月27日

衿替えの3日間は黒紋付の正装で、4日目からは色紋付になる。芸妓としての一歩を踏み出した紗月さん。ますます芸に精進し、いろいろな場面で舞妓のときより一段と厳しい要求に応えていくこととなる。洗練された立ち居振る舞い、行き届いた気遣いは人々を魅了し、やがては妹を引き、頼れるお姉さんとして、伝統をつたえていく立場となるのである。

For the first three days after Erikae, a new geiko wears a formal black kimono. After the 4th day, she wears a colored kimono with crest. Satsuki's new career as a geiko has just begun. She will strive for improving her entertainment skills as a living legacy continuing the tradition of Kagai and passing them on to the next generation.

五花街紹介

Introduction of the Gokagai

祇園甲部

Gion Kobu

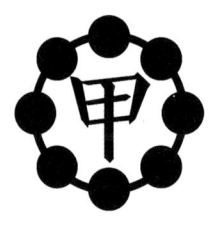

紋章について

嘉永4年(1851)、遊所御免の御沙汰があったおりの、組内八ヶ町の頭文字を円形でつなぎ、その中に「祇」の字を白抜きにした紋章に始まる。その後変遷を重ね、明治になって甲部と乙部に分かれた時、団子つなぎの中の白抜きの祇から今の「甲」に変わり現在に至っている。

※祇園甲部歌舞会：京都市東山区祇園町南側570-2
http://www.miyako-odori.jp/

歴 史

このあたりは古くから八坂神社(祇園感神院)の門前町として栄えた。江戸時代に入ってから、八坂神社や清水寺への参詣客を相手とする「茶屋」が徐々にでき始め、そこで働く「茶汲み女」「茶点て女」が次第に芸能を身につけ、それぞれお茶屋、芸妓へと発展した。寛文5年(1665)には幕府による茶屋営業の正式認可を受け(寛文10年とする説もある)た。文政年間(1818〜1830)の文献『鴨東佳話』(鴎雨山人著)には当時の祇園町の記述が見え、お茶屋の数が700軒、芸妓、舞妓の数は3000名を超えると記されている。明治14年(1881)に祇園甲部、祇園乙部(現在の祇園東)に分かれ、今日に至る。なお、祇園新橋界隈は国の重要伝統的建造物群保存地区に、祇園町南側地区は市の歴史的景観保全修景地区に指定されている。

In the early Edo period (1603-1868), many teashops opened to welcome visitors to Yasaka Shrine and Kiyomizu Temple. Gradually, the teashops transformed into ochaya and waitresses working there became geiko as they learned the art of how to entertain customers. In 1665 (some experts say it was 1670), the area received official permission from the Tokugawa Shogunate to do business as Kagai. According to a historical record written in the early 19th century, there were 700 ochaya and more than 3000 geiko and maiko in those days. The area was separated into Gion Kobu and Gion Otsubu (present-day Gion Higashi) in 1881. The area of Gion Shinbashi is designated as a traditional buildings preservation area and the area south of Shijo Street as a historical scenery preservation area.

祇園甲部組合事務所　075-561-1115　　　祇園甲部歌舞会　075-541-3391

お茶屋

安藤	清本町	中支志	富永町
一力亭	祇園町南側	イ（にんべん）	元吉町
泉政	八坂町	廣島家	花見町
池田家	有楽町	比路松	八坂町
井政	八坂町	備前屋	富永町
いまむら	有楽町	房の家	元吉町
梅の家	橋本町	福嶋	八坂町
近江作	有楽町	藤本	花見町
岡愛	元吉町	万イト	花見町
大仲	八坂町	万喜久	花見町
小田本	八坂町	松八重	八坂町
岡きみ	八坂町	松葉元	花見町
ゐ福	八坂町	丸八	末吉町
加藤	橋本町	政の屋	元吉町
貝田	花見町	桝梅	八坂町
木村咲	清本町	松田	祇園町北側
桔梗家	富永町	みの竹	富永町
京屋	有楽町	美の八重	末吉町
きねや	有楽町	みの家	末吉町
玖見	八坂町	美乃文	花町
こじま屋	有楽町	むら上	花見町
小石	八坂町	もりゐ	有楽町
大恒	有楽町	やまふく	花見町
大ヌイ	八坂町	山加代	八坂町
立花	祇園町北側	やなぎ	有楽町
ゐけ田	花町	弥す田	花見町
多麻	八坂町	よしまさ	八坂町
辻糸	花町	吉うた	花見町
つる居	八坂町	芳きし	花見町
富美代	末吉町		
冨田屋	八坂町		
登喜家	有楽町		

（平成27年4月現在）

祇園甲部・祇園東

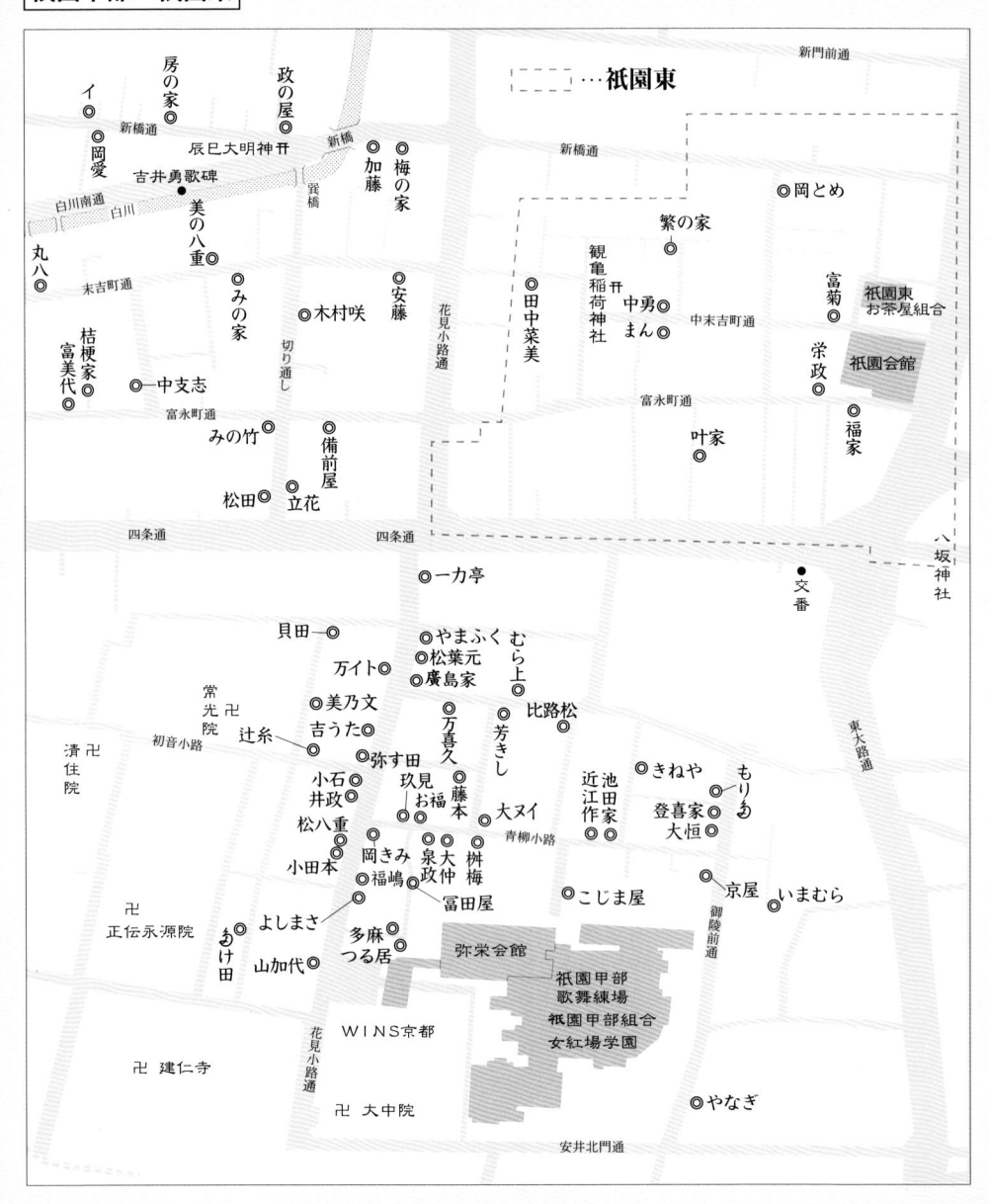

祇園東

祇園東

Gion Higashi

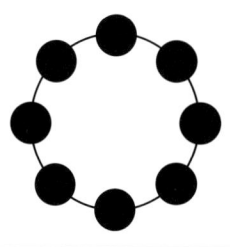

紋章について

茶店時代の由緒から、団子を八つならべた草案は、祇園甲部と同じ。明治14年(1881)の分離の際、乙部の「乙」の字がつなぎ団子の中に入っていたが、昭和30年(1955)頃、祇園東お茶屋組合となり、今日ではつなぎ団子だけとなっている。

※祇園東歌舞会：京都市東山区祇園町北側319
http://www.gionhigashi.com

歴　史

八坂神社門前の茶屋町としてはじまった祇園町は、明治14年(1881)、第三代京都府知事北垣国道によって、甲部と乙部に分けられた。昭和24年(1949)に東新地と改称され、昭和30年(1955)頃から祇園東と呼ばれるようになった。範囲としては東山区四条通の北側で、花見小路通から東大路通までである。昔、この辺りには、江州膳所藩主本多主膳正六万石の京屋敷があった。明治3年(1870)にその屋敷が取り払われると多くの茶屋が軒をならべ、華やかな花街を形成した。

The Gion area started to develop as a teashop area close to Yasaka Shrine. The third Kyoto governor in 1881 divided the area into two parts, Kobu and the Otsubu. Otsubu changed its name to Higashi Shinchi in 1949 and came to be called Gion Higashi from around 1955. Gion Higashi covers the area between Hanamikoji and Higashioji Street, north of Shijo Street. There used to be a huge residence of a samurai who governed Goshu Zeze Province (present-day Shiga prefecture) located here. The house was taken away in 1870 and a number of ochaya were newly built which emerged as a Kagai.

祇園東お茶屋組合事務所　075-561-0224
祇園東歌舞会　075-561-0224

お茶屋

岡とめ	林下町
叶家	東富永町
栄政	元町
繁の家	中末吉町
田中菜美	中末吉町
富菊	元町
中勇	中末吉町
福家	元町
まん	中末吉町

(平成27年4月現在)

宮川町

Miyagawacho

紋章について

明治中期から使用されている。三つの輪は芸妓育成機関の女紅場が府立となっており、寺社、町家、花街の三者が合流して学校施設とした記念とされている。また一説には宮川で神輿を洗ったという故事から三体の神輿を象徴したとも、宮川の「みや」を語呂の合う三輪として考案されたともいわれている。

※宮川町歌舞会：京都市東山区宮川筋四丁目306
http://www.miyagawacho.jp/

歴 史

「宮川」の名は、鴨川の四条通より南側を「宮川」と呼んだことによるなど、その由来には諸説ある。寛文6年(1666)には宮川町通が開通し、寛文10年(1670)に鴨川護岸の石積みが完成すると急速に町並みが整った。お茶屋の許可が宮川町全体に下りたのは宝暦元年(1751)である。芸能の盛んであった四条河原という地域の特色から歌舞伎との関わりが深く、歌舞伎俳優の屋号の中には宮川町の宿屋の屋号に由来するものもある。なお現在、宮川町三丁目から六丁目の市街地は市の歴史的景観保全修景地区に指定されている。

There are some stories about the origin of the name Miyagawacho, but none of them is certain. One claims that in olden times, people called the southern stream of Kamo River (lower stream from Shijo Street) Miyagawa. In 1666, Miyagawacho Street was constructed and the banks of the Kamo River were completed in 1670. As a result, Miyagawacho started to flourish and in 1751 received official permission to do business as a Kagai. The area flourished as the center of performing arts in Kyoto. It has strong connection with kabuki as Minamiza Theatre is in neighborhood. Some kabuki actor's names are related to ochaya in Miyagawacho. Today the area between the third and sixth district is designated as a historical scenery preservation area.

宮川町お茶屋組合事務所 075-561-1151　宮川町歌舞会 075-561-1154

お茶屋

いし初	四丁目
花傳	四丁目
河なみ	五丁目
川久	西御門町
河よ志	四丁目
貴久政	五丁目
きぬ家	西御門町
駒屋	四丁目
しげ森	六丁目
寿賀富	四丁目
杉きみ	五丁目
大玉	五丁目
髙よし	西御門町
たけもと	五丁目
たまや	四丁目
利きみ	西御門町
畑中	四丁目
花ふさ	三丁目
春田	西御門町
春富	西御門町
はまぐち	西御門町
藤島	四丁目
ふじ原	四丁目
堀八重	四丁目
本城	西御門町
三木家	四丁目
美津家	五丁目
湊家	四丁目
みやき	四丁目
薬師川	西御門町
雪の家	五丁目
よし冨美	四丁目
好みき	四丁目

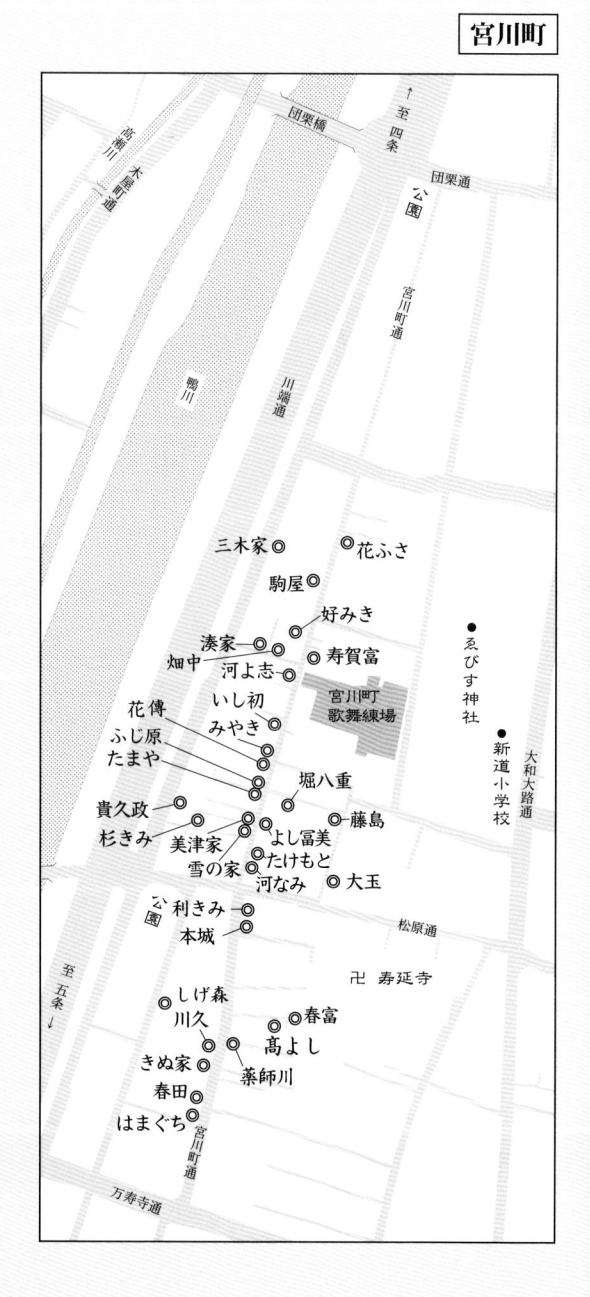

(平成27年4月現在)

宮川町

295

先斗町

Pontocho

紋章について

明治5年(1872)、鴨川をどりが初めて開催された際、創案された。モチーフの千鳥は、鴨川の冬に情緒を添える名物のひとつ。

※先斗町歌舞会：京都市中京区三条大橋西詰
http://www1.odn.ne.jp/~adw58490/

歴　史

寛文10年(1670)に鴨川大普請によって、三条通と四条通の間、鴨川と高瀬川の間に造成された新河原町通りと呼ばれた新地に始まる。高瀬川を往来する船頭や旅客を相手にした茶屋や旅籠から発展していった。正徳2年(1712)に茶屋、旅籠茶屋が認可され花街としての先斗町がはじまった。「ぽんと町」という名前の由来は諸説あり、川(皮)と川(皮)の間にありちょうど鼓のようなものなので、その音色から「ポンと丁」、ポルトガル語の「ポント」(点などの意)「ポンテ」(橋の意)がなまったもの……など様々である。

A large-scale public project around the Kamo River was undertaken in 1670 and a new street, Shin Kawaramachi, was constructed between Sanjo and Shijo Street (north to south) and between the Kamo River and Takasegawa Canal (east to west). Teashops and accommodations welcoming tourists and boatmen who transported goods along the Takasegawa Canal flourished; the area gradually developed and received official permission to do business as a Kagai in 1712. There are some stories about the origin of the name Pontocho. Some says it comes from the sound of the drum and others say that it comes from Portuguese meaning "point" or "bridge."

先斗町お茶屋営業組合事務所　075-221-2025
先斗町歌舞会　075-221-2025

お茶屋

安達	材木町
井雪	鍋屋町
上田梅	松本町
栄藤	下樵木町
籠本	下樵木町
楠	梅ノ木町
楠本	鍋屋町
さゝき	松本町
大市	若松町
田川	下樵木町
丹鶴	松本町
丹美賀	下樵木町
丹米	松本町
千栄の家	柏屋町
西里	梅ノ木町
初乃屋	若松町
福本	鍋屋町
舛之矢	梅ノ木町
松本	梅ノ木町
三芳	鍋屋町
やすい	若松町
吉富久	若松町

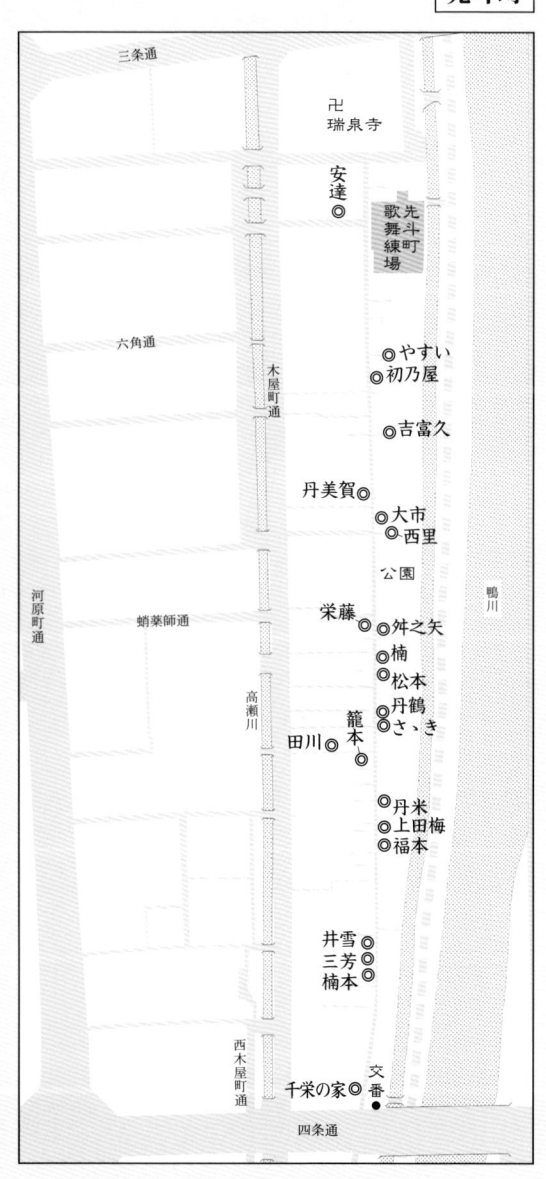

(平成27年4月現在)

上七軒

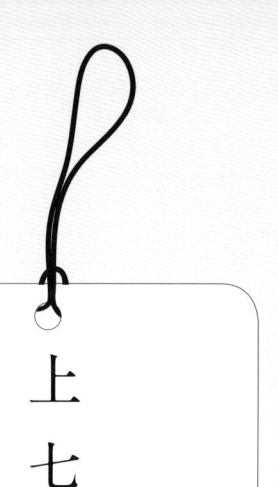

Kamishichiken

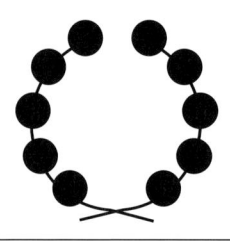

紋章について

太閤秀吉が北野大茶会を催したおり、名物の御手洗団子を献上したところ、太閤はいたく誉められ、御手洗団子を商う特権と法会茶屋株を賜った。この五つ団子の紋章はこの御手洗団子に由来している。

歴 史

15世紀中頃、北野社(現在の北野天満宮)の一部が焼失し、その修造の際に残った用材を払い下げてもらい、七軒のお茶屋を建て、七軒茶屋と称したことに始まる。天正15年(1587)、太閤秀吉が北野大茶会を催したおり、この七軒茶屋は太閤の休憩所となった。そこで御手洗団子の供応を受けた太閤はとても喜んで、法会茶屋株を公許した。一方北野天満宮には古くから巫女(神子)がいた。巫女は少女に限られたため、成熟した女性となると「茶点て女」などになったのが、上七軒の芸妓の起源といわれている。以来北野天満宮門前の花街として、また西陣に近いため、織屋の旦那衆の奥座敷として発展し、今日に至る。なお、この界隈は市の重要景観整備地区に、また上七軒歌舞練場は歴史的風致形成建造物に指定されている。

When part of Kitano Shrine (present-day Kitano Tenmangu Shrine) was burnt down in the mid-15th century, people repaired it, and seven teashops were also built nearby. These seven teashops were the origin of Kamishichiken. In 1587, Hideyoshi Toyotomi, the powerful samurai general in those days, had a big tea party in Kitano Tenmangu Shrine and the shop people welcomed him with their best care and hospitality. Hideyoshi loved it and gave them an exclusive right to do business as ochaya. Another part of the historical background is that there were sacred shrine maidens in Kitano Tenmangu Shrine. Maidens had to be young girls so that when the girls grew up they could retire and continue working as a waitress in a teashop. This is the origin of geiko in Kamishichiken. Since then, Kamishichiken has been popular with people who visited Kitano Tenmangu Shrine and wealthy merchants in the Nishijin textile district. Today the area is designed as an important scenery maintenance area and the Kaburenjo Theatre as a historically important building.

※上七軒歌舞会：京都市上京区今出川通七本松西入真盛町742
http://www.maiko3.com/

上七軒お茶屋協同組合事務所　075-461-0148　　上七軒歌舞会 075-461-0148

お茶屋

市	真盛町	大まさ	真盛町
梅乃	真盛町	大文字	真盛町
さくら	真盛町	中里	真盛町
大市	真盛町	藤幾	真盛町
大多か	社家長屋町		

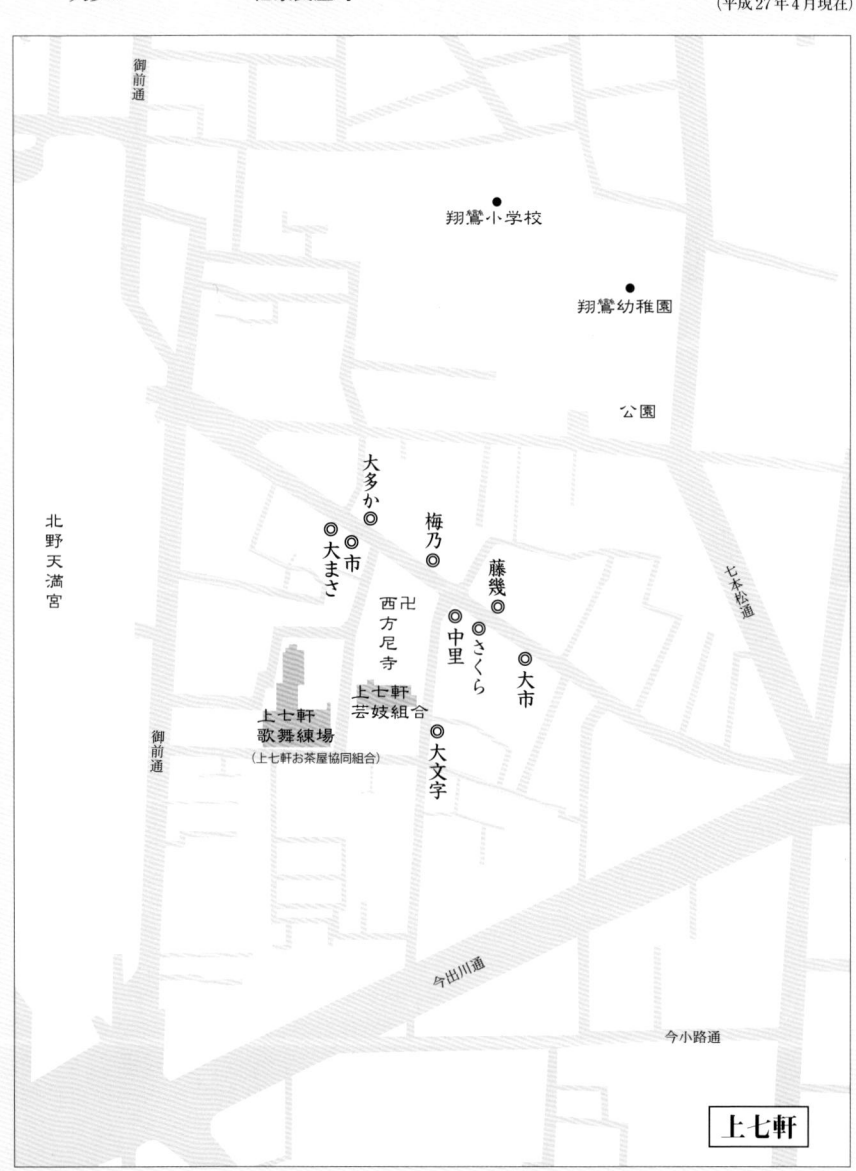

(平成27年4月現在)

公益財団法人京都伝統伎芸振興財団（おおきに財団）の紹介

平成8年に(財)京都伝統伎芸振興財団として京都府、京都市、京都市観光協会、京都商工会議所の支援のもとに設立され、平成25年からは公益財団法人として京都の五花街の伝統文化や伝統伎芸の保存継承に尽力されており、25年には京都ブランドのイメージアップや京都の都市格の向上に著しく貢献している団体として京都創造者大賞に選ばれるなど、その活動に非常に高い評価を受けておられます。

■財団の主な事業
- 京都五花街合同公演「都の賑い」を毎年6月に開催し、伝統伎芸を広く紹介し、愛好者の増加に努めておられます。
- 「弥栄会館ギオンコーナー」を運営し、舞妓の京舞をはじめ、狂言、雅楽、茶道、華道、筝曲、文楽と7つの伝統芸能を凝縮した舞台により、日本の伝統芸能の世界を広く発信されています。
- 日頃の芸舞妓の習練の発表の場である歌舞練場等の修復に対して補助金を交付されています。
- 祇園甲部「温習会」・宮川町「みずゑ会」・先斗町「水明会」・上七軒「寿会」・祇園東「祇園をどり」といった「舞台の発表」や祇園祭花傘巡行・時代祭・梅花祭等の「花街や京都の伝統行事への参加」、「伎芸の研修」のための伝統芸能等の舞台鑑賞や三味線・鼓など修繕修復等に対し、五花街に助成し、伝統伎芸の保存・継承に寄与しておられます。
- 後継者に対する伎芸の伝授・育成を奨励するため、65歳以上の伝統伎芸に従事している芸妓に対し、伎芸奨励金を支給されています。
- 伝統伎芸・技能の向上や、保存継承に努め、功績のある芸歴30年以上、かつ60歳以上の芸妓を「伝統伎芸保持者」として顕彰されています。
- 若手の芸妓が、着物などを新調する際の支援をされています。
- 舞妓姿で地元の成人式に参加し、舞を披露する舞妓を支援されています。

■「おおきに財団友の会」では趣旨にご賛同下さる方の会員を募られています。年会費は33,000円です。花街に親しみ、一層理解を深めていただく様々な特典がありますので、ぜひ友の会にご入会ください。

会員特典
1. 「北野をどり」、「都をどり」、「京おどり」、「鴨川をどり」、「祇園をどり」の各花街のをどりへの招待。
2. 京都五花街合同公演「都の賑い」への招待。
3. 五花街の芸舞妓と会員の集い「おおきにパーティー」への招待（一部会員様負担）(同伴者参加可・要会費)。
4. お茶屋の紹介。
5. 弥栄会館ギオンコーナーへの招待(会員証提示で入場できます)。
6. 会報誌をお届け。

■お問い合わせ（入会申込書請求先）
〒605-0074 京都市東山区四条通花見小路下ル　弥栄会館内
公益財団法人京都伝統伎芸振興財団　電話075-561-3901
http://www.ookinizaidan.com/

あとがき

　関東の大学を卒業した私は、京都で就職することになった。昭和47年のことである。やって来た京都は、名所旧跡が多く、見るもの全て新鮮に感じられた。休日ともなれば、趣味のカメラを片手に、一日観光に出かける。
　京都での生活が、一年過ぎた頃だ。
　その日のことは、今でもはっきり覚えている。東山界隈をそぞろ歩きし、帰りは日暮れ近かった。八坂神社から京阪四条駅に向かい、花見小路で信号待ちをしていた時だ。私の目前を日本人形かと見まごう少女が横切った。
　だらりの帯に白化粧、おこぼの音を響かせて行くのは、かわいい舞妓さんだった。初めて見た舞妓に驚いて立ち止まり、舞妓がそこにいるだけで、あたりの様子が別世界に感じられることにも驚いた。その不思議な余韻は消えることなく、仕事が終わると、夕方には祇園に足を運ぶようになる。当時は伏見区にアパートを借りていたが、電車の定期券まで買った。振り返ってみても、どれだけ夢中で写したか、我ながらエネルギーを感じる。
　花見小路の一力亭近くでカメラを構え、舞妓がお茶屋さんに向かうのを待った。時には舞妓を見かけると先回りをし、お茶屋さんの玄関前で写させてもらう。夜は即、アパートに作った暗室で白黒フィルムを現像する。中学生の頃から、好きだった写真。しかし祇園を写すことで、本当の写真の持つ面白さに気づかされた。
　昨今の写真ブームと違い、当時は舞妓の「店出し」や芸妓の「衿替え」でも、たまに居合わせた観光客が立ち止まるくらいだ。ロケーションを考え、広く町並みを入れてみたり、玄関の格子を使ったり、ノレンをくぐる瞬間にシャッターを切るなど、存分に作品作りができた。思えば至福の時間だった。
　昭和48年前後は、オイルショックがあり、経済発展など、日本全体が大きく変わろうとしていた頃だ。
　当時舞妓といえば、花街か、京都近辺で生まれ育った少女がほとんど。そのせいもあるし、女性の職業の選び方も変わったのだろう。伝統を受け継ぐ生き方は時代に合わなかったのか、舞妓さんの成り手が減った。
　祇園甲部で、舞妓さんの数が約10名に減った時、懇意にしていたお茶屋のおかあさんに言われた。
　「舞妓さんをしっかり撮っておいておくれやす。いやはらへんようになるかもしれまへんさかい」
　ショックだったが、その言葉は現実味を帯びていた。撮影に気合いが入った。花街を写真で記録し、残していこう。
　祇園甲部中心だった撮影だが、宮川町、先斗町、上七軒、祇園東へも足をのばすようになった。生活習慣、町並み、年中行事を調べ、各花街の違いにも興味がわいた。会社員だった私が、花街をライフワークに撮る写真家になるとは考えてもいなかった。しかし、花街を記録するというテーマに意義を感じた時、会社を退職した。
　写真店でアルバイトをしながら、写真家を目指してスタートを切る。幸い京都は1200年の都。撮りたい被写体は、山ほどあった。花街のみならず、風景、寺社の庭、祭など追っかけ、何でも撮った。

長く花街を写す間に、最も気をつけたのはマンネリ化だ。新鮮な気持ちを保つために、いつも自分に目標を課した。毎年、一年先の写真展会場を予約する。そして、テーマを決め、撮影する。そうすることで、一歩一歩花街への理解を深め、階段を登れると信じた。
　白黒写真で構成した初個展は多くの人々に見ていただき、作品を発表する楽しさを知った。どういう写真家を目指すかという方向を持てたと思う。その時の作品の一部を、本書、第四章に収録している。
　この個展がきっかけとなり、初の写真集『祇園舞妓抄』が出版された。そして東京のペンタックスギャラリーで写真展を開くことができた。脱サラ以後、やっと写真家としてやれると思った時の手ごたえを忘れることはできない。本当にたくさんの方々の支えあってのことだった。
　お茶屋のおかあさん、芸・舞妓さんはもちろんのこと、お世話になった方に、喫茶「たんぽぽ」のおかあさんがいる。花見小路の路地奥、古風な喫茶店は舞妓さんの密かな憩いの場。おかあさんは舞妓さんの良き相談相手で、私もカフェオーレを飲みのみ、話に耳を傾けたりした。良き時代の懐かしい思い出だ。
　写真の撮り方、内容など考えながら撮り続けると、伝統をつないできた花街は飽きることがない。芸・舞妓さんのはんなりした美を表現するため、次第にカラーポジフィルムを使うことがふえていった。ソフトレンズや特殊なフィルターをためしたり、スローシャッターや流し撮りなど、芸・舞妓さんを表現できる方法を工夫して写真集に収めた。宇治のスタジオへ二人の舞妓さんを招いたことがある。ストロボの多重露光を試みるため、暗くした部屋で舞を舞ってもらった。舞妓のしぐさの優美さと微妙な色彩の流れが美しく、「舞の輪」(120-121頁)と名付けた写真は、私の気に入りの一枚である。
　そのフィルムの時代も去り、今や、写真はほぼデジタル化してしまった。
　デジタルカメラを横目に、なじんだフィルムカメラを使っていた私も、平成18年、必要に迫られデジタルに踏み切った。この年、ワシントンDC在住の方からメールを受け取ったことによる。3月に行われるワシントンDC恒例の桜祭に作品展をし、日本大使館で講演をして欲しいという依頼だった。
　アメリカとの作品のやりとりに、私自身のやり方をデジタル化する必要があったし、世界が動いていることを肌で感じたのもこの時だ。デジタルカメラの性能が良くなり、容量も大きくなった。今では、フィルムの使用がなくなり、データー処理もパソコン。写真展の作品も自分のプリンターでできる。一枚の作品のために、たくさんの工程が必要だったことを考えれば、隔世の感がわいてくる。デジタルカメラの容易さ、楽しさが、人々を引きつけ、写真を楽しむ人口を増やしたのだろう。
　花街を訪れる人は、近年、驚くほど増えた。祇園の花見小路あたりは、行事のある時など写真愛好家たちでふくれあがる。撮りたい気持ちは、痛いほどわかる。しかし各花街の芸・舞妓さんは、毎日芸事の稽古、お座敷など時間いっぱい励んでいる。花街のいい雰囲気を保つためにも、そこで暮らす人々への配慮をお願いしたいと思う。

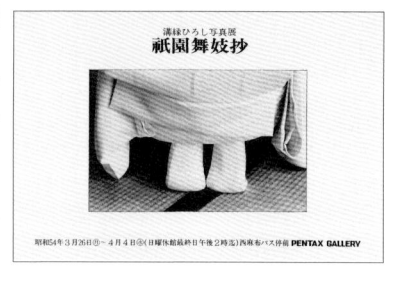

302

一昨年、京都市が花街を「京都をつなぐ無形文化遺産」として選定した。長い間ライフワークとしてきた花街が、このような指定を受けたことは本当にうれしい。おもてなしの文化の極みというべき花街が、よりすばらしくなるよう願っている。私もまた、花街を写すことで記録し続けたい。

　本書は、これまで写した五花街の写真を、たくさん掲載した。年中行事、舞台、一人の女性の舞妓から芸妓への記録、そして初期の白黒写真など。私が40年以上花街を撮ってきた、今までの集大成だと思っている。

　この出版にあたり、各花街の歌舞会、お茶屋組合、そしておおきに財団など、多くの関係者の方々にご協力をいただきました。本書に登場していただいた芸・舞妓さんにも、この場を借りて御礼申し上げます。特に第五章は「美しいキモノ」の芸・舞妓連載企画のために、取材撮影した写真を中心に構成しました。一緒に取材していただいたハースト婦人画報社の吉川明子氏にも、重ねて御礼申し上げます。また、光村推古書院の大西律子氏にも、きめ細かいご配慮をいただきましたこと、心より感謝いたします。

2015年4月吉日　　溝縁ひろし

溝縁ひろし（みぞぶち　ひろし）

1949年、香川県に生まれる。1971年、千葉工業大学卒業後、株式会社ユニチカUGに入社。1975年、同社を退社し、スタジオ勤務を経てフリーの写真家になる。1980年、写真事務所「PHOTO-HOUSEぶち」設立。1994年にJPS関西展運営委員長をつとめる。2000年と2002年には京都・キルギス国際写真交流会代表として独立記念日に国立美術館で作品展。現在、京都の花街を中心に撮影を続けており、京都の四季や祭、四国八十八ヵ所、西国三十三ヵ所など様々なテーマに取り組み、また海外取材や、海外での写真展（アメリカ・ワシントンDC、ドイツ・ミルテンベルク）など国際交流も積極的に行っている。

日本写真家協会会員、NHK文化センター京都写真教室講師

ホームページ　http://www.h-mizobuchi.com

個展

1979年「祇園舞妓抄」東京ペンタックスギャラリー
1990年「四国霊場　花・巡礼」富士フォトサロン（大阪）
1995年「KYOTO・ぎをん・舞妓」富士フォトサロン（東京）
1999年「霊場遍歩」富士フォトサロン（大阪）
2000年「京逍遥」キルギス国立美術館
2000年「祇をん・市寿々」京セラ・コンタックスサロン銀座
2002年「『写真日記』を楽しむ」ぎゃらりぃ西利
2005年「番外も巡る四国へんろ」高松市美術館市民ギャラリー
2006年「京都花街に伝わる伝統美」ワシントンDC　日本大使館
2006年「京都・花街・芸舞妓」富士フォトサロン（東京・大阪）
2008年「写真と仏画で巡る四国33所」奈良国立博物館
2009年「先斗町界隈」ギャラリー古都
2010年「祇をん多満葉」ギャラリー古都
2011年「霊峰富士『芸者』ドイツ・ミルテンベルク旧市庁舎
2012年「花街の伝統美」東海東京証券1階ギャラリー（東京）
2012年「ミルテンベルクの町と人々」ドイツ・ミルテンベルク市
2013年「京舞妓 宮川町」ギャラリー古都
2015年「『祇をん・紗月』…舞妓から芸妓へ…」ギャラリー古都
他多数

出版

1978年『祇園舞妓抄』（吉村書房）
1985年『祇園―今に生きる伝統美』（日本交通公社）
1987年『写真日記』自費出版
1992年『花へんろ』（保育社）
1995年『京舞妓歳時記』（東方出版）
1997年『四国八十八ヵ所・花遍路』（新潮社）
2000年『祇をん・市寿々』（小学館）
2002年『京都 花街』（光村推古書院）
2004年『はんなりと―京舞妓の四季』（京都新聞出版センター）
2004年『西国三十三ヵ所物語』（東方出版）
2006年『四国八十八ヵ所』（主婦の友社）
2007年『重森三玲』（京都通信社）
2010年『決定版・先斗町』（淡交社）
2010年『京都五花街』（光村推古書院）
2012年『法然上人の言葉』（淡交社）
2013年『京舞妓　宮川町』（光村推古書院）
2014年『四国遍路道 弘法大師伝説を巡る』（淡交社）
他多数

■協力
祇園甲部組合／祇園甲部歌舞会／祇園甲部芸妓組合
宮川町お茶屋組合／宮川町歌舞会／宮川町芸妓組合
先斗町お茶屋営業組合／先斗町歌舞会／先斗町芸妓組合
上七軒お茶屋協同組合／上七軒歌舞会／上七軒芸妓組合
祇園東お茶屋組合／祇園東歌舞会／祇園東芸妓組合
公益財団法人京都伝統伎芸振興財団（おおきに財団）

恵美須神社
祇園畑中
祇園祭山鉾連合会
祇園丸山
北野天満宮
京都四條 南座
切通し進々堂
源光庵
平安神宮
八坂神社

株式会社実業広告社
株式会社青龍社
株式会社ハースト婦人画報社「美しいキモノ」編集部

（順不同・敬称略）

京都の花街
―芸妓・舞妓の伝統美―

平成27年6月22日　初版1刷　発行
平成31年3月16日　　　　3刷　発行

写　真　溝縁ひろし
発　行　合田有作
発行所　光村推古書院株式会社
　　　　604-8257
　　　　京都市中京区堀川通三条下ル 橋浦町217-2
　　　　PHONE075-251-2888　FAX075-251-2881

印　刷　ニューカラー写真印刷株式会社

本書に掲載した写真・文章の無断転載・複写を禁じます。
本書に掲載した文章の著作権は全て執筆者本人に帰属します。
本書のコピー、スキャン、デジタル化等の無断複製は著作権法上での例外を除き禁じられています。本書を代行業者等の第三者に依頼してスキャンやデジタル化することはたとえ個人や家庭内での利用であっても一切認められておりません。

乱丁・落丁本はお取り替えいたします。

デザイン　辻恵里子（ニューカラー写真印刷）
進　行　山本哲弘（ニューカラー写真印刷）
英　訳　大久保彩（アドブレーン）
編　集　大西律子（光村推古書院）

The Kagai in Kyoto
– Legendary Beauty of Geiko and Maiko

First Edition June 2015
First Printing June 2015
Third Printing March 2019

By Mitsumura Suiko Shoin Co., Ltd.
217-2 Hashiura-cho Horikawa Sanjo
Nakagyo-ku, Kyoto 604-8257 Japan

Photographer: MIZOBUCHI Hiroshi

Publisher: Mitsumura Suiko Shoin Publishing Co., Ltd.
Printer: New Color Photographic Printing Co., Ltd.

Design: TSUJI Eriko (New Color Photographic Printing Co., Ltd.)
Program Director: YAMAMOTO Takahiro
　　　　(New Color Photographic Printing Co., Ltd.)
Translator: OKUBO Aya (AD BRAIN INC.)
Editor: OHNISHI Ritsuko (Mitsumura Suiko Shoin Publishing Co., Ltd.)

All rights reserved. No part of this publication may be reproduced or used in any form or by any means, graphic, electronic, or mechanical, including photocopying, recording, taping, or information storage and retrieval systems, without written permission of the publisher.

ⓒ 2015　MIZOBUCHI Hiroshi　　Printed in Japan
ISBN978-4-8381-0526-7